Once Upon a Time...
at the
Missouri State Fair

My maternal Grandmother, Laura Sophia Louisa nee Harms Chehaski with her escort, Claus Wenig, at the 1909 Missouri State Fair. They rode the train from Lincoln, MO to see the great Dan Patch, the Iggorote Village and to tour the new John Deere building with the latest in farm machinery and carriages.

By
Dianne Peck

Copyright 2002 by Dianne Peck
ISBN 0-9723249-0-9

All rights reserved. This book, or parts thereof, may not be reproduced in any form without permission.

Published by
Down on the Creek Publishing
Rt. 3 Box 3207E, Lincoln, MO 65338
(660) 668-3803

Printed in the United States

Introduction

The Early Days

How old is the Missouri State Fair? Not to long ago not many could have answered that question. But now if anyone has been paying any attention at all, they should know that the annual grand event is celebrating 100 years of fun.

In this fast paced age, great things come and go so speedily that the events of yesterday are overshadowed or forgotten by contemplation of those of tomorrow and next week.

Back in the beginning, the land was donated by the Van Ripper family who had originally set this land aside for the location of the state capitol. When the seat of government remained steadfastly in Jefferson City that thought was abandoned. It was given as the State Fair site and the Missouri General Assembly passed a legislative act to establish a State Fair. Sedalia became the successful contestant for its location after vying against other towns for its designation.

The never to be forgotten beginning was in 1901 and the gates were thrown open and the public viewed their first annual exhibition. To say that it was crude by today's standards would be an understatement. It was virtually a prairie tent show. Meager appropriation, excessive heat and drought had hampered the work needed to be done. It was described by those attempting to open the show as heartbreaking and soul trying.

The grounds as we know them today was almost as nature had created it. There was plenty of elbow room for man and beast. At the end of that first week a storm broke out and scattered tents and their contents over the prairie. But it was a good fair beginning and they forged on. In 1903 they had a fire that originated in the cattle barns, spread to the Fire Department Building and the temporary grandstand. All was destroyed. Other disasters were to occur through the years but everyone always carried on with optimism.

Full appreciation of how far we have come will hopefully be demonstrated by this book. It is not an in depth history but a condensed version, told in what I hope is a simple style with much nostalgia in the many pictures.

Street Car (circa 1910)

Getting to the Fair

In 1901, just prior to opening day of the Fair, there appeared in the local paper an announcement of a decision by the board, "the board rescinded a rule charging for vehicles or horses to the grounds, and country people will be glad to know that they will not have to pay extra for driving or riding within the enclosure."

In 1902, the Fair Director was disturbed when he learned that many people were unable to obtain transportation to Sedalia, and that crowds were left at nearby towns because they could not get on the trains. The special trains could not even bring all that wanted to come. Several trains were sent out from Sedalia to the nearby places and returned loaded, with others still waiting to come.

But over the years the train service evolved into a smooth running business. Special round-trip tickets were offered with complete schedules of not only the boarding time at your "home" station but the arrival time at the fairgrounds. Also included was the time you could expect to return home that evening.

Before the construction of our interstates, the train service was essential in getting to the Fair. St. Louis Day and Kansas City Day always drew large numbers arriving from the respective cities.

The street car line was a popular means of getting to the grounds by local Sedalians; although it was not available the first year. An announcement in the paper on August 9, 1901 stated that the outlook for an extension of the street car line to the fairgrounds was not good. Manager Osborne of the line was not prepared to say that it would be constructed that fall. However the report continued, that the Missouri Pacific and M.K.&T would run trains from the city

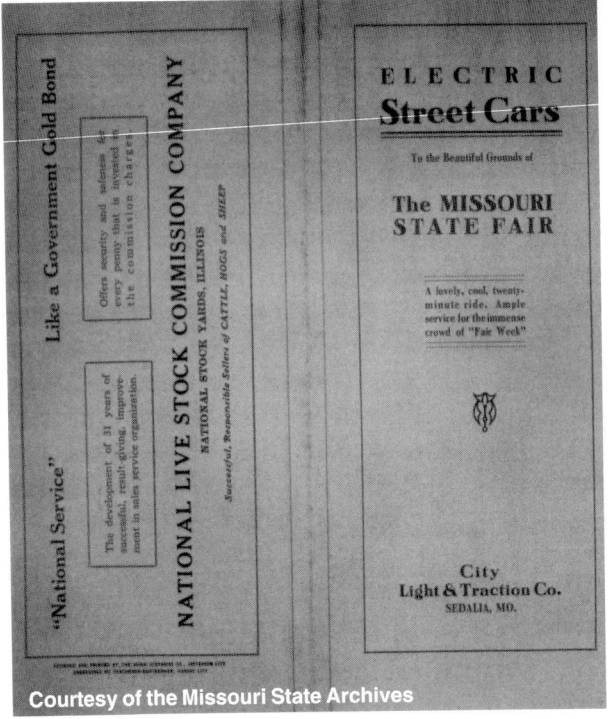
Street Car Ticket

every few minutes and the Fair Directors felt confident that the crowds would be handled in a satisfactory manner.

Hazel Lang in her "Life in Pettis County" spoke of the street cars and told of the various routes taken around the city. I quote, "Later the cars went to the fairgrounds on Ohio to 16th and 16th to the front gate at State Fair Boulevard. During the Fair, the West Third Street line turned on Limit to go to the fairgrounds."

In the depression time of the early 30's The automobile had a big effect on how many customers actually still used the street cars. Many people had no money and walked. The bricks were to be taken up by the WPA to repave Third Street and the Ingersoll Co. was ready to give up the street car business as it was broke. So the WPA took up the tracks along with the bricks and the little street cars were no more!

The late 40's and early 50's saw Olen and Marvin Howard owning and operating a bus service in the city. It was a losing proposition as more and more people drove their cars and the few that depended on bus service were not sufficient to make it a paying proposition. The fare was 10 cents and they featured special ads in the paper reminding people that they had special routes going to the fair and back all day. They featured a picture of their drivers in the "Fair ad", resplendent in their uniforms.

Sedalia has always been a railroad town. This miniature train displayed by Bryan Wakefield of Des Moines, Iowa was here in 1934.

But I doubt if anyone has ever made a greater effort to arrive at the Fair than a young man named Henry Harbaugh. In 1911, on the day President Taft spent at the Fair, the young boy rode a mule bare back from Bedford, Missouri, a distance of 175 miles. He then put the mule through a number of amusing antics on the mile track in front of the grandstand. The lad would offer a sum of money to anyone who would stay on the mule's back. He found no takers! Probably because the mule bucked, reared up and plunged sideways. All this seemed to be at the boy's command because at times the long eared animal was as docile as a lamb. No further account was found of Henry and the mule's antics. One would assume that they returned home by "shank's mare" just as they arrived.

This Street Car would have ran on the East Side of Sedalia - The Sign at the top states 13th Street & East Sedalia (circa 1910).

The sign on this Street Car read Ohio, 16 & Grand Av. (circa 1910).

"	7:40 a. m.	LEXINGTON		"	9:40 p. m.
"	7:50 a. m.	ARGONNE		"	9:30 p. m.
"	8:00 a. m.	TABO		"	9:25 p. m.
"	8:10 a. m.	PAGE CITY		"	9:18 p. m.
"	8:17 a. m.	CONFEDERATE HOME		"	9:13 p. m.
"	8:45 a. m.	HIGGINSVILLE		"	9:10 p. m.
"	8:59 a. m.	AULLVILLE		"	8:57 p. m.
"	9:15 a. m.	CONCORDIA		"	8:45 p. m.
"	9:25 a. m.	EMMA		"	8:35 p. m.
"	9:35 a. m.	SWEET SPRINGS		"	8:25 p. m.
"	9:50 a. m.	HOUSTONIA		"	8:10 p. m.
"	10:02 a. m.	HUGHESVILLE		"	7:55 p. m.
"	10:17 a. m.	GEORGETOWN		"	7:40 p. m.
Ar.	10:30 a. m.	SEDALIA		Lv.	7:30 p. m.

Between WARSAW and SEDALIA

Going
August 16, 17, 18, 19, 20

Returning
August 16, 17, 18, 19

Lv.	7:00 a. m.	WARSAW		Ar.	10:00 p. m.
"	7:20 a. m.	SCHUYLER		"	9:29 p. m.
"	7:38 a. m.	LINCOLN		"	9:12 p. m.
"	7:50 a. m.	TAHOMA		"	8:57 p. m.
"	8:10 a. m.	COLE CAMP		"	8:41 p. m.
"	8:32 a. m.	MORA		"	8:25 p. m.
"	8:44 a. m.	SPRING FORK		"	8:11 p. m.
"	8:54 a. m.	VALDA		"	8:02 p. m.
Ar.	9:10 a. m.	SEDALIA		Lv.	7:45 p. m.

Between JEFFERSON CITY and SEDALIA

Going
August 16, 17, 18, 19, 20, 21

Returning
August 16, 17, 18, 19, 20, 21

Lv.	5:30 a. m.	JEFFERSON CITY		Ar.	10:45 p. m.
"	5:37 a. m.	COLE JUNCTION		"	10:35 p. m.
"	5:43 a. m.	SCOTT		"	10:29 p. m.
"	5:49 a. m.	ELSTON		"	10:24 p. m.
"	6:00 a. m.	CENTERTOWN		"	10:17 p. m.
"	6:08 a. m.	McGIRKS		"	10:08 p. m.
"	6:12 a. m.	BRANT		"	10:04 p. m.
"	6:20 a. m.	CALIFORNIA		"	9:58 p. m.
"	5:31 a. m.	CLARKSBURG		"	9:46 p. m.
"	6:42 a. m.	TIPTON		"	9:35 p. m.
"	6:50 a. m.	DOW		"	9:27 p. m.
"	6:53 a. m.	SYRACUSE		"	9:24 p. m.
"	7:05 a. m.	OTTERVILLE		"	9:12 p. m.
"	7:15 a. m.	SMITHTON		"	9:00 p. m.
Ar.	7:30 a. m.	SEDALIA		Lv.	8:45 p. m.

Train No. 37 will be held at Sedalia from Monday to Saturday, inclusive, until 6:00 p. m.

See Local Agent for full particulars

ROUND TRIP TICKETS
ON SALE
AUGUST 13 TO 21, 1920
INCLUSIVE

FINAL RETURN
LIMIT
AUGUST 23, 1920

C. L. STONE, Passenger Traffic Manager, Saint Louis

SECURITY PRINTING CO. OF ST. LOUIS

"Partial 1920 Train Schedule for surrounding towns to the Fair"

Y'all Come

Y'all come to the State Fair this year
   'Cause its going to be mighty fine,
With high school bands for you to hear
   And Missouri's best cattle and swine.
Shown will be sheep and mules and goats
   By farmers today and tomorrow,
And there will be yells from the barkers' throats
   For girl shows or chambers of horror;
While mother looks at the cakes and the pies
   The cooks have displayed there with pride
Junior will beg with tears in his eyes
   To go on a carnival ride.
But mother will wander on and just look,
   If she's smart she'll take along a few comics
So her youngster can look at his favorite book
   While she views the home economics;
And father will see the machinery display,
   The team pulling contest and races.
No family agrees on exactly the way
   To go to the Fair - nor the places;
Missouri exhibits of wild life and fish.
   The railroad exhibit of trains;
Just saunter around and see what you wish,
   Vegetables, fruit, honey and grains;
There's archeology, hobbies and flowers,
   There's poultry, rabbits and cheese,
Fine arts, you can just look for hours
   At any exhibit you please;
The grandstand events both day and night,
   Highway Gardens where friends always meet
And the church this year will be a delight
   With its music sacred and sweet;
Antique machinery, Ozark Jubilee,
   Square dancing for those who would dance,
The Stars Over Ice is something to see
   And the horse show where fine horses prance;
The busy hum of all kinds of noise,
   Humanity there is a mass,
From those very old to wee girls and boys
   Of every description and class;
But that makes the Fair and down you will sit
   To watch all the people go by,
It's something tremendous you'll have to admit-
   The carnival lights 'gainst the sky,
The kid with the hot dog, the man with a cane,
   The teenagers holding hands
People dressed up and others quite plain,
   The squawking that comes from the stands,
Oh, this is the Fair - The Missouri State Fair,
   Y'all Come - for who'd want to miss -
The one big state show in which we all share -
   There nothing all year quite like this.

                                       Hazel N. Lang

Ms. Lang wrote for the Sedalia Democrat and compiled a history of the area in 1973. This poem was in the Sedalia Democrat August 22, 1955.

Admission Prices

One hundred thousand free admission tickets to the 31st Annual Fair were distributed throughout the state. It was the Fair Board's aim to give the citizens of Missouri outstanding exhibitions at a price which would bring the annual educational event within the reach of everyone. These special free tickets were good for admittance on four special days. The free ticket was accepted when used with one fifty cent admission ticket.

The board in that year (1932), also reduced the automobile parking from 50 cents to 25 cents. Similar reductions were made in fairground activities all along the line. It was a large effort to bring people out to the event in the depths of the Great Depression when money was tight or totally non-existent for some.

Entrance to State Fair, Sedalia, Mo.

Courtesy of Trenton Boyd Collection

Main Gate

The main gate to the fairgrounds off 16th Street is not the original but has been there since 1939. It is described architecturally as being Art Deco/Art Moderne and its original construction cost was $4,500. There are three individual ticket booths spanned by steel arch work that contains the Missouri State Seal and the words Missouri State Fair. The some what larger middle unit was designed with a small bath room. The booths are no longer used.

The study done for the historic register nomination claimed the architect to be Arthur J.P. Schwartz. An interesting picture and story in the August 18, 1952 *Sedalia Democrat* told it another way. The picture was labeled with the caption: "Charlie Botz's Gate" and the photo showed the gate being used for the first time in 1939. Charlie Botz was driving the first car through the portals. The story went on to say that the gate was not officially named for the Sedalian but it was Mr. Botz's idea for the location, size, general appearance and accommodations. He supposedly had talked about it for years with several fair secretaries and finally Charles Green "gave in" to Mr. Botz's plan and the gate was constructed.

Mr. Botz had been featured the previous year in 1951 as being the perennial fair visitor. He had apparently only missed one fair since it's beginning in 1901 and that was because he was in the hospital with appendicitis. His wife argues and says he has missed two but he disputes that, as only being confined to the hospital could have kept him away. Mr. Botz told the paper that he likes to get a box at the grandstand, one way back. He gets there early before the crowd starts and looks his fellow Missourians over as they come in. He stated that they were the greatest comedians in the world. "They do the funniest things, wear the funniest clothes, and I wouldn't miss the show of the people for anything." He continued on that he was always the last out of the grandstand because it was so entertaining to watch the people leave.

There are many things that draw us all back to the fair year after year and the study done by the historic preservation in 1991 claimed that more than a billion people had entered the fairgrounds since the first fair in 1901.

Maps of the Missouri State Fair

1905

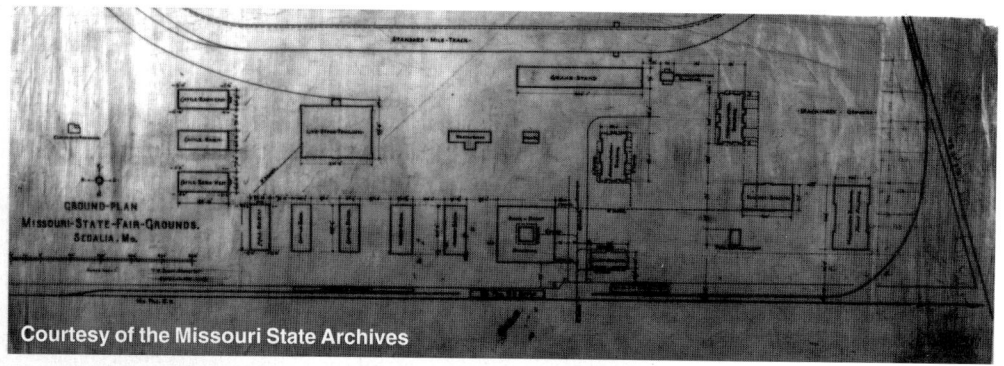

Courtesy of the Missouri State Archives

Although these maps are hard to read, they give us a really good idea of how much construction took place during the 1905 and 1910 Fairs.

1910

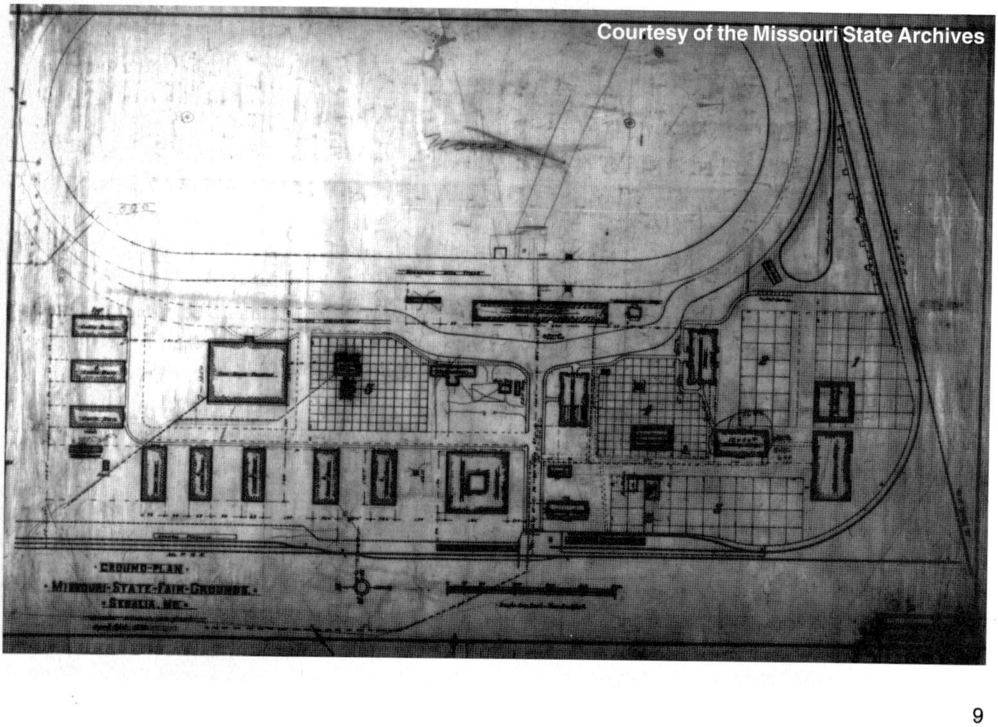

Courtesy of the Missouri State Archives

1937

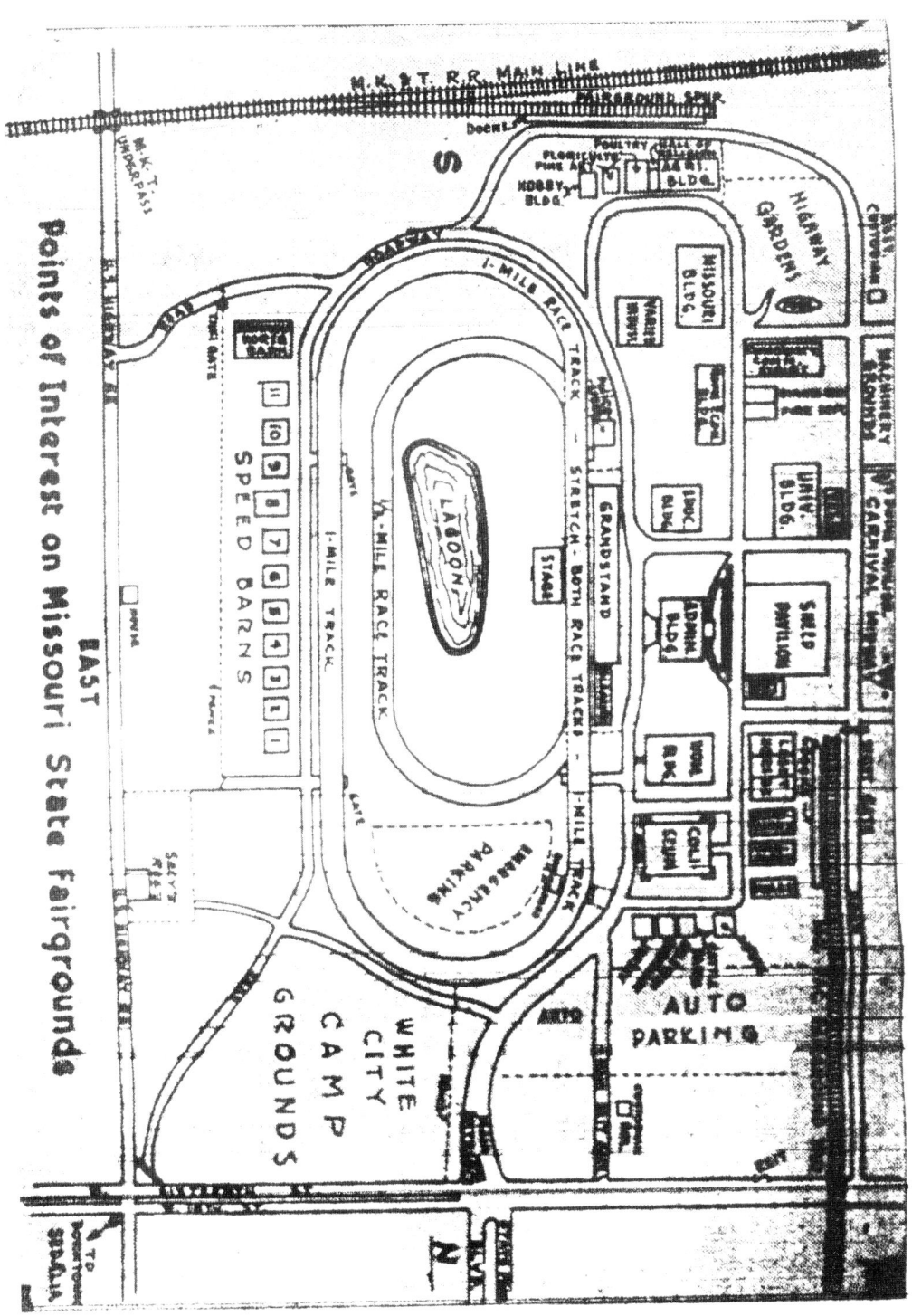

1951

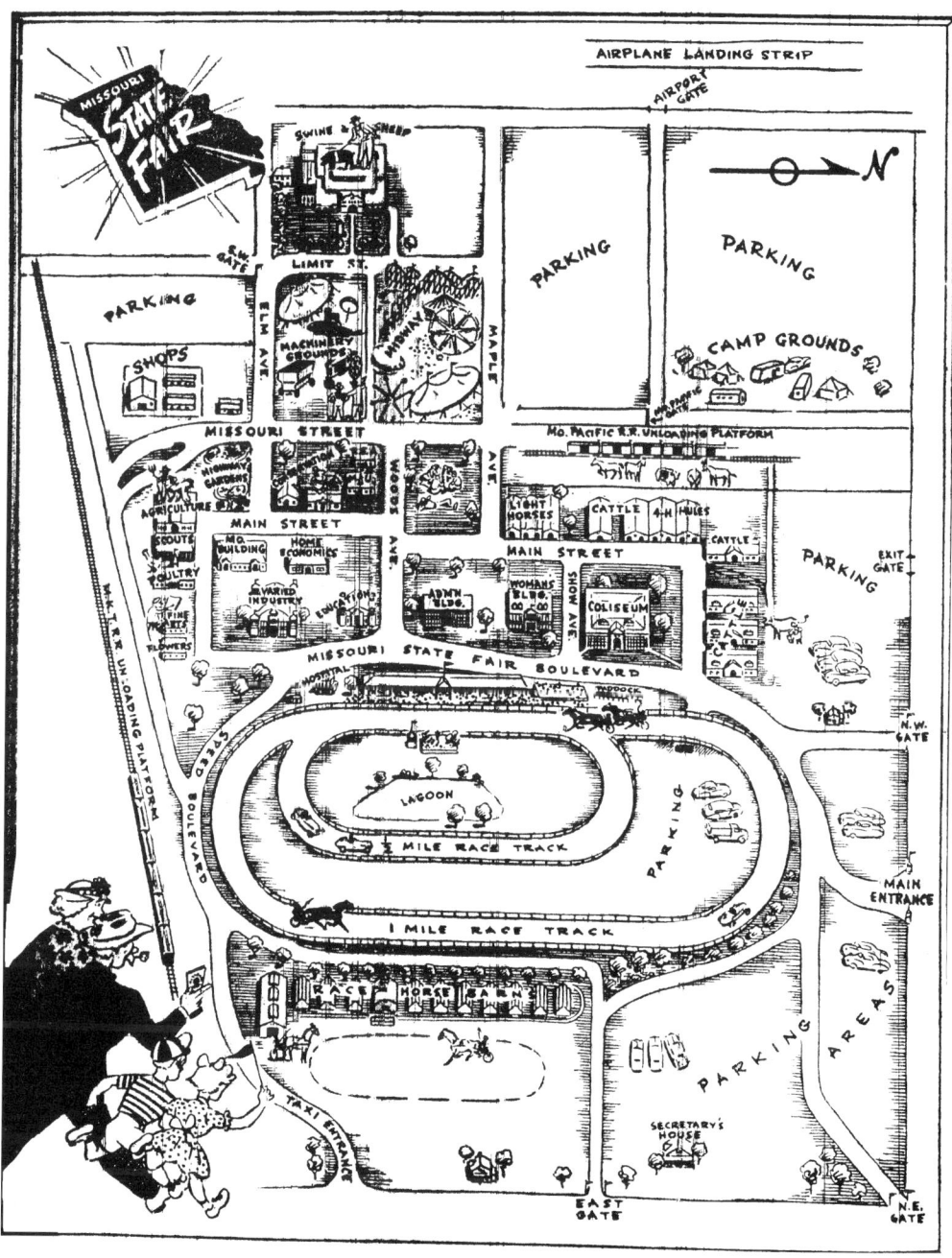

2002 Missouri State Fairgrounds Legend

1. Administration Building .... Page 25
2. Agriculture Building .... Page 45
3. Cattle Barns .... Page 55
4. Charolais Barn
5. Coliseum .... Page 17
6. Commercial Building .... Page 28
7. Conservation Building .... Page 53
8. Dairy Center .... Page 14
9. Donnell Barn
10. Donnelly Arena
11. Draft Horse Barn
12. Farm Bureau Building
13. Feed and Forage
14. FFA Building .... Page 77
15. FFA Children's Barnyard
16. Fine Arts Building .... Page 46
17. Fire Station
18. First Aid Station
19. Floriculture Building .... Page 46
20. 4-H Building .... Page 78
21. Frisco Engine Display
22. Grandstand .... Page 33
23. Hereford Barn .... Page 55
24. Highway Gardens Building .... Page 50
25. Highway Patrol .... Page 52
26. Home Economics Building .... Page 56
27. Horse Barns
28. Log Cabin
29. Maintenance Building
30. Mathewson Exhibition Center
31. MEC Building
32. Mo-Ag Theatre
33. Missouri Frontier Building .... Page 54
34. Mule & Draft Horse Barn
35. Personnel
36. Plumbing/Electrical
37. Poultry & Rabbit Building .... Page 49
38. Sheep Pavilion .... Page 81
39. Shorthorn Barn .... Page 55
40. Simmental Barn
41. State Fair Arena
42. Swine Pavilion .... Page 82
43. Ticket Office
44. Varied Industries Building
45. Womens' Building .... Page 26
46. Youth Building
● Public Restrooms
xxx Fencing

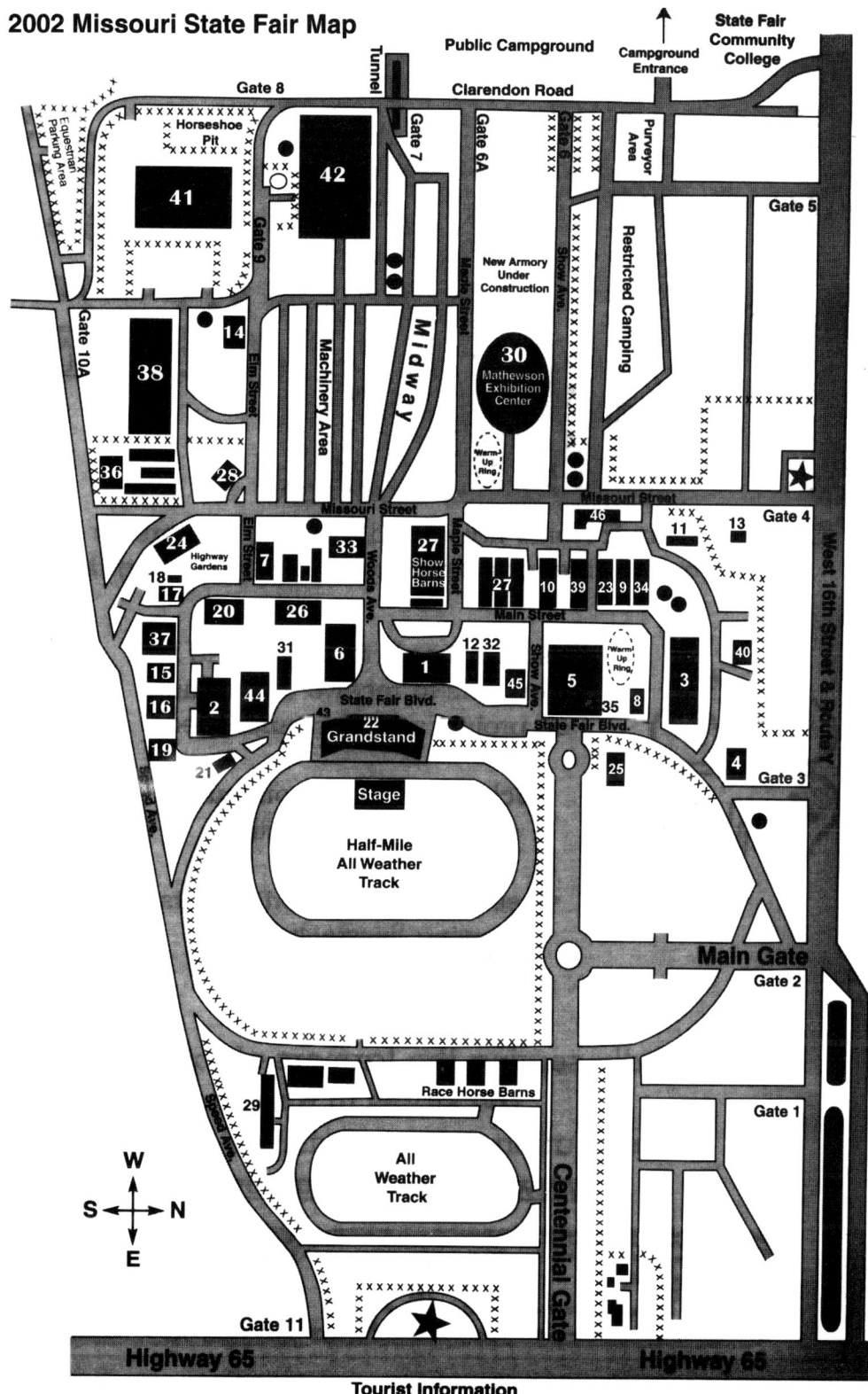

Poster from the 1920's

Dairy

One of the principle commodities of Missouri's diversified agriculture has always been the dairy industry. From the earliest beginnings of our State Fair, the dairy people showcased their products. The Guernsey barn was erected in 1905 and that same year the dairy people assumed the (now FFA) building from Poultry. In 1907, the Jersey barn was completed and that same year *The Sedalia Democrat-Sentinel* reported on the extensive exhibits of butter and cheese. 40% of the cheese factories from around the state were represented and 20% of the butter manufacturers. The bulk of the dairy butter exhibit came form the farmer's wives around Sedalia. The ladies were in brisk competition and were determined to display their considerable abilities.

A walk through description included the many booths that exhibited cream separators. Also on hand was Mr. Cline, State Dairy and Food Inspector. He was addressing the subject of adulterated food products and that it not only cost people money but sometimes their health. The greatest feature was a milking machine made by B.L.K. Co. of Little Falls, New York. The machine operated beside a platform built up three feet high on which stood four cows. Regular milking demonstrations were shown at 3:30 a.m. in the morning and 5:30 p.m. in the afternoons. Mr. Lewis of St. Louis County was on hand to demonstrate and answer questions. He used these machines daily on his own farm at home.

By 1909 the Dairy Association had a membership of 1200 and was hoping for continued growth as they estimated there were at least 40,000 dairy farmers in the state. A test had been devised by Stephen Babcock, an American Agricultural chemist, that evaluated milk by butterfat content. This high butterfat content probably inspired the famous "cow race" held in the 20's by the State Dairy Commissioner at the Fair. The Jerseys and the Holsteins each had separate races. By 1926 the Holstein barn had been completed and the industry would see the breed come to the forefront for production.

Dairy Superintendent, Joseph Stakes, announced at the 1951 Fair that Missouri had become the second ranking state in cheese making and the fifth in butter production. He stated that there were six plants located in Missouri that would make fifty-four million pounds of cheese foods. And in honor of this the champion twenty pound wheel of aged cheese would be presented to Missouri's Chief Executive, Forrest Smith, on Governor's Day. The "Daisy" of cheese had been produced by the Emma Creamery Co. of Emma, MO.

In 1954, the Dairy Bar was erected where the REA Building stands now. Dairy products were featured items on the menu, along with hot dogs and hamburgers. It was air conditioned and a great spot to rest. There were various displays showcasing dairy products, not the least of these being "Elsie the Cow". Elsie was molded from solid butter and reigned supreme on the north wall in her own cooler. Her popularity with the kids at the fair ranked up there with Smokey the Bear and Otto the Talking Car. Unfortunately the talented lady that created Elsie each year was unable to carry on the tradition by 1998. About 1957, visitors to the fair could watch cows being milked by machinery in the "milking parlor". Original cost of the structure was $9,780. The building was shaped like a mobile home and had a small dairy bar attached to the south end where fair goers could purchase milk, ice cream, etc.

In the late nineties, C.C. "Bud" Gerken became the impetus toward the construction of the present day dairy facility, just north of the coliseum. In 1998, the State Legislature set aside $162,000 for its construction. The entire building cost was $300,000 so the gap in funding was raised by allied dairy groups. The new facility was greatly needed as the existing edifice was how dairying had been done in the 50's. The viewing of a cow being milked had become such an object of interest that the dairy barn now has a State Fair Dairy Herd operated by a contracted vendor, Veronica Gatton of Crane, MO. She has various breeds and conducts an educational "talk" for the public while the cows are being milked. The importance of the facility was summed up by MO Ag Director, John Saunders, when he said, "The building showed it from the cow to the cone."

Sedalia vs. St. Joseph

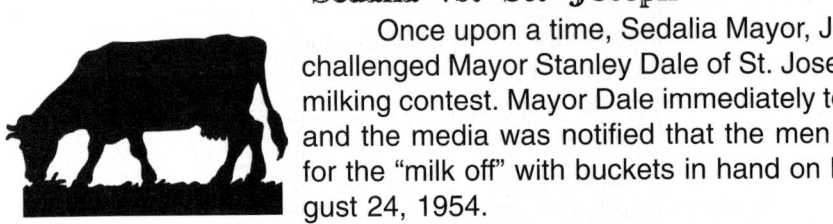

Once upon a time, Sedalia Mayor, Julian Bagby, challenged Mayor Stanley Dale of St. Joseph, MO to a milking contest. Mayor Dale immediately took the dare and the media was notified that the men would meet for the "milk off" with buckets in hand on Monday, August 24, 1954.

Both men were "working" with Grand Champion Jerseys. Mayor Dale's animal was "Valiant Checkmate Loretta" owned by C.O. Deal Jersey Farm of St. Joseph and Mayor Bagby had "Brampton Design Faye" belonging to Earl Wood of Smithton, MO.

Mayor Charles Schumaker of Bellfountain, St. Louis gave the "go" signal and the race was on. Bagby balanced himself on a milking stool and soon showed the crowd why he was in the milking business. The milk began to stream while Mayor Dale was getting milk but in smaller streams.

Now both Mayors had large cheering sections and one of Mayor Dale's fans, a woman, stooped down on the other side of the cow to help "her mayor" out but Sedalia's Police Chief, Edgar Neighbors, soon put a stop to the assistance.

Lloyd Evans, KWOS Radio of Springfield, was the master of ceremonies. Mayor Hubert Morgan of Memphis, MO and Mayor Louis Dierken of Concordia, MO served as the weighing officials. In the five minute contest time, the boy from down on the farm, Julian Bagby, proved his mastery in the art of hand milking a cow when he weighed in with 7.5 pounds of milk. Mayor Dale drew 2.7 pounds. Mayor Bagby was presented a championship ribbon and a two pound roll of Longhorn cheese. A large crowd was drawn for the event and was touted as entertainment at its best.

Livestock Pavilion Coliseum 1905-1906

The Coliseum - The Fairgrounds Center Piece

The monster livestock pavilion was dedicated on October 2, 1906 and from its beginning seemed to set a whole new tone for the Fair. Historical accounts tell us that the weather was made to order and the livestock and horse shows were the best. Participants were encouraged to enter by the improved surroundings. From the outset, much thought was given to the design of the building with its architecture complementing that of the nearby cattle barns. And although its magnificent structure has heard politicians speechifying and performers entertain it has always remained a horse and livestock judging arena for more than ninety years.

When President Taft's train made its debarkation at the fairgrounds in 1911, the committee would have breakfast waiting for him at 8 o'clock sharp in the Director's Building. Then promptly at 9:30 a.m. he would proceed to the Coliseum in order that he might address the people. He spent twelve hours viewing the various aspects of Sedalia and the Fair and departed on the Presidential train for Kansas City.

Four years later, former President Truman came to the Ham Breakfast as the featured speaker and awarded the trophy for the Grand Champion Ham. After breakfast he strolled through the livestock barns and viewed some of the livestock judgings inside the Coliseum. He partook of lunch, enjoyed some harness races and went back to Independence. I'm not positive but he probably took the train. Mr. Truman traveled by train a lot.

Now both of these Presidents visited the fairgrounds and the grand old Coliseum in some degree of calm. But when President Reagan made a two hour whirlwind trip here in 1984, the entire town and area surrounding it was gone over with a fine tooth comb. Security was tight, there were farmers with nasty placards, heckling and verbal accusations stating that he was selling the farmer down the river, set the mood. One of the more pleasant moments came when Governor Bond presented President Reagan with one of Missouri's famous Grand Champion Hams. This was directly before Reagan spoke and attempted to moderate the tone. The coliseum was full and it was encircled with the huge crowd outside. Unfortunately the speakers outside failed to work and the speech went unheard by those on the exterior of the building.

Reagan fans lined the back doors of the mule barn hoping to get a glimpse of the President. This created the one really good laugh of the day. Not used to such large groups of people milling around, the mules kicked up dust and were restless. The joke of the day became, "They're not used to that many Republicans!"

Hoofbeats From the Past

In 1984, a bit of the past thundered into the Coliseum. And no matter where they go they are always crowd pleasers. I speak of the 1st Calvary Division of the United States Army. No they are not ghosts, they are real. I too thought that the mounted calvary that rode over the rise just in time to save the endangered wagon train was extinct. They are not. But nowadays their only adversaries are watermelons and burlap straw filled bags. This is an elite group that are hand picked from over 10,000 men and women in the First Calvary Division. They perform at fairs and events such as the Cotton Bowl and were part of the Inaugural Parade for President Reagan. They were in Sedalia the week he also appeared at the Fair. Maybe Reagan did too many Death Valley Days segments and wanted them here for back up.

When the show is in progress they have sabers drawn and rush at full gallop toward their target, the repulsive burlap man. He is toppled from his perch as they thunder on to spear targets dangling from ropes. Then the mounted soldier scoops up a "pony soldier" from the ground, who swings up behind him without stopping.

Different comments from the troopers about pre-show jitters included butterflies before performing, like riding a big roller coaster and you're always nervous! Mark Twain explained their particular brand of courage when he said, "Courage is resistance to fear, mastery of fear, not the absence of fear." They all agreed that if you let something get to you, you could mess up the whole show. They said they didn't really notice the crowd because when the adrenaline is pumping you are in another world.

Even their horses are brave. If a horse flinches or shies from swords or gunfire, that won't do. They prefer a bay horse or a dark one because that is tradition. It became tradition because a light colored horse was easy for Indians to spot. Everyone in the outfit takes care of his own horse and grooms them for shows. And not only is their riding style traditional, so is their uniforms with wide brimmed hats. Even their weapons are authentic or authentic reproduction.

This outfit came into being in 1972 in order to keep the Calvary traditions alive. They are a big part of the Army's public relations effort. They were quite impressive as they toured the grounds daily but their prowess in the Coliseum during horse show intermissions was tremendous. This was a select group of men that graced the Fair that year and to put a slight twist to Longfellow's words, "You cannot look into the past, it is gone. You can improve the present, it belongs to you. And young man go forth to meet the shadowy future without fear and with a manly heart". Somehow watching those manly hearts perform made me proud to be an American. And just maybe we need an encore performance.

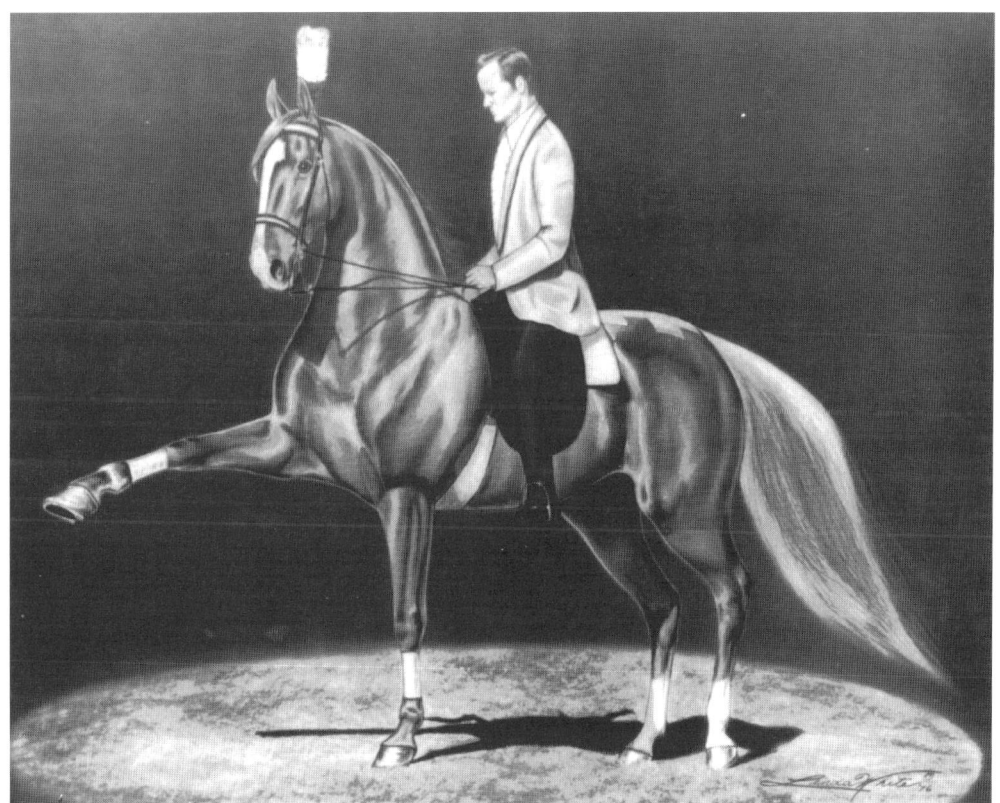

This lovely painting of Mr. Rythm hung on the wall of State Fair Restaurant when it was owned and operated by Gene and Marion Landon. Mr. Wallen had asked Gene to display it, along with a multitude of other fair memorabilia that graced the walls of the dining room.

Mr. Rythm - The Dancing Horse

He did the Rumba, Missouri Waltz, Mexican Hat Dance, the Hula, Spanish Trot backwards, pirouette and over 53 other dance steps and tricks. He was Mr. Rythm, the world's greatest exhibition horse. When his owner and trainer,

Darrel Wallen, was on his back, Mr. Rythm would delight and thrill the audiences as he performed the most fantastic dances and tricks that you would ever see any horse do.

His owner, Darrel Wallen, began trying to teach the equine at the age of two to be a five gaited show horse. Mr. Rythm had his own ideas of what he wanted to do in the ring. When Wallen attempted to teach him to rack (a fancy show step), the horse would rear up. When discipline didn't help, Wallen got the idea that the horse was trying to tell him something. Wallen insisted that Mr. Rythm really wanted to dance. And dance he did, better than any horse in the country. He became the star in every horse show he attended.

Wallen raised the horse and had many of the horse's relatives but none of them could even imitate him. There is no value that can be put on an animal like him, a horse like him comes once in a blue moon. Wallen said that it would take most horses four years to learn what Mr. Rythm had down perfect in seven weeks. The horse had walked 380 feet on his hind legs. He had broke the previous record of 150 feet.

The horse was featured in *Reader's Digest, National Geographic and Sports Illustrated* to name a few. They would travel 100,000 miles a year to perform. Wallen said the horse was in his element when he had an audience and that he was a real ham.

The horse had performed at major events all over the United States including the Missouri State Fair. Their home, when not touring was in Sedalia. The horse weighed 1100 pounds and stood 16 1/2 hands high. Wallen named him Mr. Rythm when he began dancing and although the spelling is incorrect that's how Darrel Wallen wanted it. "He's different, so I wanted the spelling different!" was Wallen's explanation. I was never privileged to see this magnificent animal in the flesh but many did, once upon a time at the Missouri State Fair!

Politicians at the Fair

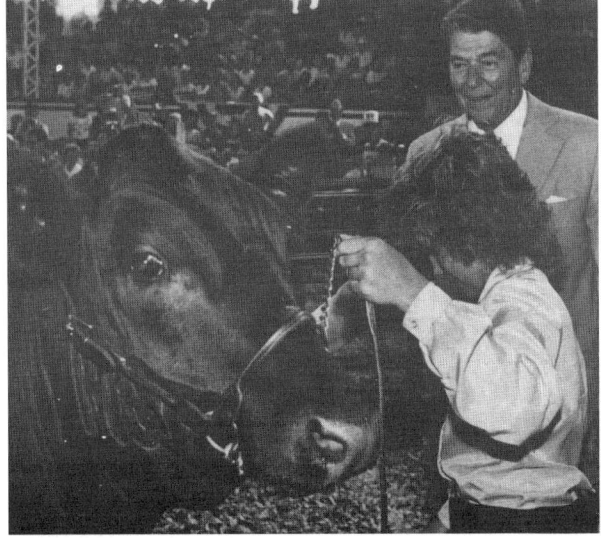

In 1984, President Reagan visited the Fair.

Courtesy of Marion Landon Collection

This was Truman's favorite photograph of himself. He loved being shown at the Missouri State Fair with two champion mules. He and others often compared him to a mule, not always in a flattering manner from his opponents. That is probably what caused him to quip about this picture, "By the way, I'm the one on the left."

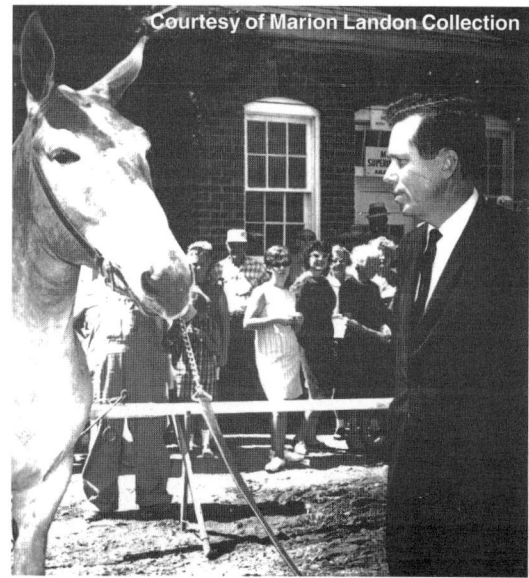
Courtesy of Marion Landon Collection

Governor Warren Hearnes poses with a mule in this picture. I don't think Missouri politicians considered it politically safe to come to the Fair and not be photographed with a Missouri Country Ham or a mule. Mules and politics have always been intertwined in Missouri. Our own Mark Twain once told that he had a mule who would kick up his heels when Twain told him a joke. He said he introduced the mule to a politician and the mule kicked down the barn in laughter.

Missouri Governor Mel Carnahan waves to visitors during a parade at the opening of the 98th Missouri State Fair, in 2000. Seated with him in the back of the convertible are, center, Gary Slater, Director of the Missouri State Fair and Lowell Mohler, Chairman of the Missouri State Fair Commission. The driver is Norwood Creason, a member of the Fair Commission.

Success and Fame

To know the difference in success and fame was to know Tom Bass and Loula Combs. Success was Tom Bass and Fame was Loula Long.

They say that Loula Long Combs' first complete sentence was, "Buy me a pony." Her father, millionaire lumber baron, Robert A. Long, did just that. Loula as a young woman had the family stables full and overflowing. So her father built Longview Farm which gave Loula plenty of room to keep and train horses.

Tom Bass, a black man born into slavery, was a special man that delighted thousands in this country and abroad with his amazing feats of horsemanship. Tom came into this world in 1859, the son of a slave girl, Cornelia Gray and her owner, Wm. Hayden Bass.

Although Tom and Loula came from opposite ends of the social scale, they shared a life long passion for breeding and training horses. For almost 65 years, her horses won ribbons in this country, Canada and England. She was known as "Queen of the American Royal", where she made a yearly appearance well into her 80's. To please her audience, she always wore a dazzling hat as she drove her carriage around the show ring.

Tom Bass was not an aggressive person. He was shy and quite modest by nature but he captured the admiration of other show people and horse audiences equally. He many times was subjected to racial slurs but he discovered early in his career that the best way to even the score was to win. By the time Tom was in his twenties, he was held in high regard as a horseman that could solve the problems with horses that the best had given up with. One of his secrets was to use the proper bit on the horse. He designed a bit and it caught on quickly. The Tom Bass Bit is still used today but he never made a nickel from its design because he never patented the design. Invented over a hundred years ago, the Tom Bass Bit has never been off the market.

His color was not unnoticed, but neither was his record of wins. In fact it became a symbol of achievement to have beaten the "colored boy". Tom was finally able to open his own stable and he needed a "brag" horse. So he brought in a gray colt named Columbus. He and Tom became famous together. Later Tom would sell Columbus to Buffalo Bill Cody.

Tom Bass died in 1934 and when he lay ill shortly before his death he reflected on the so called demise of the horse. *"I'm glad automobiles came in when they did. They have emancipated the horse. Many a night I have lain awake thinking about poor tired horses that had been whipped all day to make them do things that their bodily strength did not permit. To a man that loves a horse, to see one abused is as bad as having the whip laid on his own body. So the automobiles after all were a relief to the average horse. Good horses are still with us and are commanding a higher price than ever before. Riding is a more popular sport today than it was twenty five years ago when almost everybody had a horse. It will always be popular because there is nothing that can compare in thrills with a swift canter on the back of a horse."*

Tom was known and respected by Will Rogers, Teddy Roosevelt, Grover Cleveland, August and Adolphus Busch, the Armour, Cudahy and Swift families as well as the Vanderbilts. He was well know by William McKinley and was invited to ride in Queen Victoria's Diamond Jubilee Parade.

The International reputation of Miss Loula Long attracted celebrities and Presidents too. In 1911, at the age of thirty, she and her family went to England. Loula entered her horse in London's Olympia Horse Show. She returned by October to attend the 1911 Missouri State Fair. She arrived in her special railroad car "Kymokas". The name represented the abbreviations of the three states her Father had lived in. The paper also noted that the famous Tom Bass of Mexico, MO was on hand with his prize winners too. Miss Loula had brought Beaucaire, Revelation and "The King". Tom Bass brought Bernice B, Rex Chief and Columbia Girl.

The Fair goers of 1911 had already been treated to a visit from President Taft, some of the largest and finest exhibits since its inception, and now they were to witness the two most influential luminaries in the horse world. The Coliseum was standing room only, the horses had been lined up to be photographed when a near panic resulted. A flash from photography equipment ignited streamers and paper decorations. The flames were threatening to spread to other decorations. Calmer heads in the group prevailed on the excitable spectators to remain seated. The blazing decorations were cut loose and dropped into the show ring doing absolutely no damage. And the show carried on.

Tom Bass and Loula Long worked with horses whose names even yet today mark the breed. Tom Bass had no documentation of his own birth, yet he was a dominant influence in an industry in which lineage and papers were of the greatest importance. Loula came from luxury and prestige. Yet, to steal a line from Will Rogers, "St. Peter will no doubt admit Tom Bass on horseback." I say he opened the gate to Loula in her little Roadster, pulled by Revelation and wearing the most spectacular hat of her entire career. And just think, they were here together in 1911 and it happened once upon a time at the Missouri State Fair!

Courtesy of the Missouri State Archives

50 Years Together

Mr. and Mrs. George Robert were celebrating their 50th year of marriage when they posed for this picture at the 1950 Fair. Mr. Roberts was a contender in the evening horse show.

Administration Building

This is the original Administration Building, as you can see it housed several departments. It was headquarters for the Highway Patrol. This structure was originally on the south end of the grandstand in 1901. But was moved in later years to the east side by the Speed Barns. The Speed Barns were the structures used to house the race horses. Due to lack of funds for restoration the Administration Building was razed in 1979.

In 1946 it became the Hospital and Speed Office Building. Doctors and nurses were on duty day and night during the fair. Officials of the speed department were headquartered in this building, which was also used as sleeping quarters for the State Highway Patrol.

In 1926-27 the Administration Building we have now, was designed by Bast. The contractor was Dean & Hancock. The building remains relatively unaltered from its earliest times. In addition to offices, it contained bedrooms which were installed for members of the fair board of directors and a cafeteria. In 1964, the building was remodeled (inside) in order to bring the plumbing and electricity up to modern standards.

Courtesy of the Missouri State Archives

In its last years the old original Administration Building served as the office for the Speed Department.

Womens' Building

Womens' Building, State Fair Grounds, Sedalia, Mo.

Courtesy of Dianne Peck Collection

The Womens' Building is a three story building. The third floor was equipped with cots, mattresses, rest rooms and showers. It served as living quarters for girls who were members of visiting high school bands. Alterations over the years include the removal of a one-story rear wing during renovations in 1965 and the installation of a wheel chair ramp. Note the fenced play yard provided for youngsters not yet old enough to enjoy the fair.

Circa 1910-1911 T.W. Bast, a Sedalia architect, had designed all of the fair's massive red brick buildings and pavilions. But unlike the "male" accommodating structures previously built, this one was to be molded to mirror Missouri Womanhood. Perhaps a more realistic explanation, a male concept of those feminine qualities. The building was intended to look and be like "home". It was a common belief of that era that women and children needed domesticity to endure. So unlike our parks of today which encourage family togetherness, that era demanded that the sexes and ages be segregated.

One of the temporary structures on the fairgrounds in it's first years was the Missouri Ladies Club tent for women. In May of 1908, the Executive Committee of the State Fair Board voted unanimously to recommend to the state legislature to receive funding for three new buildings on the fairgrounds, one was to be a Woman's building. The board called the existing conditions "deplorable" and went on to say that the state should surely be able to do better for its women and children.

In official correspondence on the subject there was a letter describing a bathroom or comfort station problem that arose when an unusually large number of ladies attended the fair on a certain day. The lack of sufficient toilet facilities was finally solved by the ladies themselves. They, in groups would form "human circles", facing outward, with the lady seeking relief in the center. This situation was undoubtedly what induced the gentlemen to describe the arrangements as "deplorable"!

The self-satisfaction in the new structure and in their "women folk" of the state was voiced in the article that appeared in the Missouri Ruralist, October 12, 1912.

The Missouri State Fair is one place where the tired "mother of seven" can go for a day of pleasure and really enjoy herself. The State of Missouri believes that the mothers of its sons should be assured the same good time as any other citizen, which doubtless accounts for the little demand for equal suffrage made by Missouri women. In the center of the fairgrounds stands the Womens' Building. Large, costly and imposing it stands as a monumental tribute to the women of a great state. In it are large rest rooms filled with comfortable couches for those unused to the arduous labors of sight-seeing. Other portions are devoted to culinary exhibits and conference halls. Upon the walls of the reception rooms hang beautiful pictures. Every woman within the grounds is here "at home".

But best of all, in the rear of this from the din of the Fair, is the nursery and playgrounds for the babies and youngsters. Within a cool shaded room are to be seen dozens of tiny ones, who, under the care of competent nurses, are far safer and more comfortable than they could possibly be in their mother's arms.

The sight of this day nursery would warm any human heart.

Outside in a playground surrounded by a high wire netting, children old enough to play are having a good time, far surpassing that of their absent parents. With shouts and chuckles, they teeter and swing and romp, perfectly oblivious of the fact that they are at a State Fair, which they are not old enough to enjoy, nor strong enough to see without "dragging".

A glimpse of these scenes and a visit to the Womens' Building is enough to assure even the most skeptical that there is no reason why anyone should not see the Fair and that the great State of Missouri looks after the comfort of its women folk and the kiddies.

In addition to serving as a rest area for women and children, the building has housed fine arts exhibits, lectures, music competitions and a cooking school. Up until about 1990 the building was partially occupied by senior citizens groups. In 1990, the State Fairgrounds made a cooperative arrangement for long term use of the building by the Department of Natural Resources (DNR) and it will now be used for exhibits and educational activities year round.

Commercial Building

This ancient post card from 1911, depicts the present day Commercial Building as the Textile and Art Building. It was one of three red brick buildings constructed for the 1903 Fair.

When the Fairgrounds was declared a Historic District and placed on the National Register in 1991, the paper work states that it was originally the Agriculture Building and was redesignated as the Education Building by the 1920's. Sometime later it became the Commercial Building. A building for Missouri business people to display their wares, such as McLaughlin Brothers Furniture store in the late 40's or early 50's. The public was unable to purchase cars, appliances or furniture during the war years and now with the availability of such products, such a display held great interest for the consumers.

Every housewife could envision entertaining guests in this up to date living room. You can see the corner of the modern dining room on the right side.

A kitchen such as this was every woman's dream!

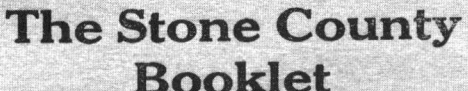

The Stone County Booklet

A Guide to Prosperity and Happiness

FOR FREE DISTRIBUTION

—At The—

MISSOURI STATE FAIR

August 20th to 27th, 1927

Published by the Business Firms and Farmers
Of Stone County, Missouri

Printed and Bound by the
NEWS-ORACLE, Galena, Mo.
CRANE CHRONICLE, Crane, Mo.

County Displays

For many years individual counties had displays in booths that touted their individual assets and why you might possibly wish to live there. Pettis County always had a large agriculture exhibit while other counties would stress minerals, etc. This booklet is an example of literature handed out to interest future prospects. In this 1927 publication the booklet named towns and their population and churches. Recreation and dairying were named as prospects for income and it even featured a profile of their farm agent, Mr. George Hawn of Ozark, MO.

There were not the winners in the pretty baby contest. It was the Blue Ribbon Baby Contest, which was held in the Women's Building. The contestants were not only judged for a "pretty face" but overall health and an outgoing personality.

Posing for the picture from left to right: Mr. and Mrs. Leo Leiter with Virginia Sue (9 point girl - red), Mr. and Mrs. Wm. K. Gibson with Kathryn Ann (Blue Ribbon girl), Mr. and Mrs. John K. Anderson with Vincent Ray (9 point boy - red), Mr. and Mrs. Glenn Smith with Glenn Lee (Blue Ribbon boy)

Media

Back in 1906 it came to the attention of the fair directors that something had to be done about their weak relationship with the newspaper industry. The following press bureau note gave them a wake-up call. *"A street fair or carnival of some sort is going on at Sedalia this week."* This was printed by a St. Louis daily paper and the other leading papers of Kansas City displayed about the same amount of information and interest in our State Fair.

The media have become welcome guests and have been on hand for some very memorable moments. Visits from three presidents, pretty girls, ham breakfasts filled with back room politics, tornadoes and the Hickory County tornado - Sally Rand with her fans, have given them ample to talk about and write about.

One of the most colorful radio personalities ever was C.C. Williford. He began his career at KWTO in Springfield, MO in 1933. While speaking at the fair he told the story about a certain farmer that was well known for his accuracy in weather predictions. A group of politicians in Washington D.C. came out to interview the farmer. When asked about the secret of his forecasting he replied, "I don't mind telling you. See that donkey out there in the field? When he grazes contentedly the weather will be good. Whenever his tail is swinging, I know it is windy. When the end of his tail is wet, I know there is dew. When its wet, I know it's raining. One morning I got up and his tail was gone and I knew we had a tornado." C.C. continued on that the big wigs had gone back to Washington amazed and satisfied - and promptly appointed a jackass to be head of every weather bureau in the country. His punch line to the story was, "It just proves that weather forecasters have an even lower standing in the community than a politician." I have no idea how many times he appeared at the Fair but he was always a welcome addition.

During President Reagan's visit to the fair in 1984, a press pool was set up at State Fair Community College's Yeater Building. In addition to the regular press coverage that the fair usually receives, the entire press pool that constantly follows a President needed lots of phones to call in stories to their anxiously awaiting editors.

In 1951, Don Davis, the President of WHB Radio out of Kansas City, told a little story about the State Fair and President Calvin Coolidge. Davis was a publicity man for the Missouri State Fair back in the early twenties when radio was in its infancy. The fair was to be officially opened that year with the voice of Calvin Coolidge, President of the United States. He was to be broadcasting from Washington D.C. All this was to demonstrate the wondrous marvels of radio. Everything was set. People were listening and the Fair people waited, but nothing happened. Minutes passed, everybody was on edge. The voice just didn't come. "What will we do?" asked someone. "I know what I'm going to do" said Davis and he went to the microphone and started talking. He opened the Missouri State Fair and nobody knew the difference.

Media Coverage (Circa 1960's)

Grandstand

President Taft and party watching the various performances on the track from the grandstand in 1911.

The present day grandstand was built in 1968 and is a conglomerate of steel and concrete. Many think that it replaced the original grandstand. It didn't. The original grandstand of 1901 was a last minute temporary structure. The reason being made note of in the August 9, 1901 paper. *"There has been some delay in the erection of the steel grandstand. This being caused by the steel workers strike. The amphitheater should be erected now but instead of that only two car loads of material have been shipped, and not a piece of it is yet on the ground."* The contract had been let to the Midland Bridge Co. of Kansas City and a representative had arrived that afternoon to explain the cause of the delay. Three days later the Fair had hired a Mr. Hammond to construct a temporary wooden grandstand at the fairgrounds and he had promised to rush it forward to an early completion. The decision was made to go with this and then immediately dismantle it when the fair was done the next month so that the original steel amphitheater could be erected for next year.

The Midland Bridge Co. was to have had the steel grandstand completed by August 8 but didn't due to the steel workers strike. They were unhappy with the action of the fair directors in declaring the contract void. The company representatives had made an attempt to enter the grounds but were refused admittance. He told the press that his company would lose $5,000 if they were not allowed to go ahead and erect the stand. The Bridge Co. man had reconsidered a few days later and said that he would not attempt to interfere with the erection of the temporary stand. He said that they would store the materials his company had ordered and would attempt to later renew the contract.

The racetrack was begun in 1900 and *Sedalia Democrat* reporters were surprised at the sight of a small army of laborer already at work on the grounds, getting things ready for the first fair the next year. *"Menefee & Heck, the contractors, had a force of 25 men at work at the southeast end of the sight, excavating and grading for the mile long track. An immensely large Western wagon loader and elevating grader, drawn by 16 horses and operated by four men, was moving up and down the place where the excavating was being done for the track. The machine is a wonder. It not only rolls on wheels, but it cuts a straight line into the earth and plows and loads the dirt into wagons at the same time. Besides the grader, ten teamsters are at work hauling away the dirt and filling in places which cover the route of the track. Mr. Heck stated that the job was an immense one, and that it would take until cold weather in which to complete the race course. During that time thousands of tons of dirt will have to be removed from the race track and used to fill up places that are now below grade."*

But there must have been a few hitches in the race track too, because the following summer in July 1901 this story was released. *"This has been an extremely hot and dry summer. Farmers report that their fields are not producing one bushel of corn and here in Pettis County the potato crop is a complete failure. They are rushing completion of the racetrack at the fairgrounds, using hundreds of teams and slips. This pushing in the extreme heat is causing the deaths of dozens of horses."*

Well it was all finished in time to open the gates the first time and the racetrack remains an important part of the Missouri State Fairgrounds. Although originally designed for horse races it was soon being used for auto racing as well. They later added a track within a track. The half mile track added versatility and satisfied the public's appetite for speed events.

Through the years many unique shows and attractions have been seen. And seen better after 1946, when the track before the grandstand was under flood lights for the first time in the Fair's history. It would take good lights to see the tiny 18 inch diameter dance floor that was on a pole 125 feet above the ground. Benny and Betty Fox did an unbelievable number of stunts and steps on their little dance floor in the sky. The routine included waltzes, rumbas, jitterbugging and acrobatic dances. They thrilled the crowds at the grandstand in 1951 with every performance.

A water ballet was another feature of the 1951 fair before the grandstand nightly. Water effects created by fountains and the ever changing lighting with especially arranged music gave something different to Missouri State Fair goers. The show was back in 1954 with everything bigger and better than before. It was billed as dancing waters and had first been done in Europe, specifically Germany first and then later in America at Radio City Music Hall. It gave the illusion that the water was playing the music. Spectators said they never tired of going back time after time, that it seemed to be an entirely new show. I guess the promoters were dead serious when they chose for that year the slogan, "Fun Galore in 54".

Colonel L.M. Monsees, one of the world's most famous mule breeders put on quite a program for Taft back in 1911. He had mules stringing out almost the entire length of the mile long track. The group was led by little Miss Mary Jones astride a small mule, decorated with bunting and many unique slogans appeared on banners and placards on the vehicles in line. The appearance of a team of large mules towing a disabled automobile had a banner that read, "This is what you will have to resort to when your engine dies." This brought forth lusty cheers from the grandstand. Then Colonel Monsees appeared astride "Orphan Boy" on a wagon decorated with golden rod and greenery. President Taft smiled and applauded as he read the slogan. "On our way to success. Now all together."

Over the years we have seen a change in the tastes of the public. And nowhere is it more evident than in the entertainment they seek. In 1959, Gene Autry appeared along with the Manhattan Rockets (dancers) and it has slowly evolved from Porter Waggoner on to Willie Nelson to Hank Williams Jr. But no matter who is performing in front of that grandstand it's just like the slogan said the year Gene Autry appeared, "A Whale of a Time in 1959".

A racing bill from the early days

Auto Races

I'm sure no one would believe that there were auto races at the very first fair back in 1901, but there was. The announcement was as follows. *On Monday, September 9, there will be an exhibition on the mile track of automobiles, which will include the various kinds propelled by gas, electricity, steam, naptha and gasoline. On Tuesday there will be a mile race between horseless carriages! Wednesday will be a half mile race and fancy automobile track work. Thursday will be the two mile race by automobiles. Friday will be a fancy automobile track exhibition. Bicycle races will be sandwiched between the automobile races as follows: Tuesday, a mile and a two mile bicycle race. Wednesday, a half mile bicycle race and a tandem bicycle race. On Thursday, a one mile, open bicycle race and a two mile tandem bicycle race followed on Friday with half mile and mile bicycle races.*

A short note in an area paper in 1919 announced that in the auto contest, Harry Geutzer, in a Teucelot in the free for all race, had made ten miles in 9:46 and broke the state record.

As the auto came more and more to the forefront, all types of auto racing became more and more popular at the fair. From the large crowds in attendance, it was evident that it was a popular event. In 1965, there was an estimated crowd of 10,000 in the grandstand watching the time trials for the 100 mile stock car race when one of the cars left the track and slammed into the fence. There was a large crowd of spectators along the outside of the fence and had only a few seconds before been warned over a loud speaker system to leave the area. He told them they were in a restricted area which was closed to spectators. The spectators were lined up against the chain link fence on the south end of the grandstand. They had crawled under a fence to get into the closed off area. Many of them were children. An eyewitness account came from a Missouri Highway Patrolman, a nine year veteran. W.D. Ryan from St. Louis said that it was the most horrible sight he had ever witnessed. He described the scene as men, women and children crumpled and scattered about the ground. Some were crying and others were moaning. Someone heard a woman scream and the car went into the crowd without turning out of the straightaway at 12:45 p.m. One of the first ambulances on the scene was from Whiteman Air Force Base which was taking its turn at duty that day. All of the ambulances from Ewing, Gillespie and McLaughlin Funeral Homes were pressed into duty and rushed the injured to Bothwell Hospital. Doctors and nurses not on duty, who had heard about the accident, started arriving to augment the staff already on duty. Four persons died at the scene and two priests from St. Patrick's and Sacred Heart, respectively administered Last Rites. They also helped to console family members of the dead and injured. Bill Crane, Liberty, MO, driver of the 1964 Dodge stock car was not among the injured. The final toll was four persons killed and fourteen injured by the stock racing car that was thrown out of control by a tire blow out.

In 1957, Sonny Roberson of Windsor, MO plunged his car through the fence on the south turn of the race track and flipped off a 10 foot embankment. Thankfully, Roberson was uninjured.

Courtesy of the Missouri State Archives

Various funeral homes in the area formerly provided ambulance service for the public. Today ambulance service is a speciality. The local funeral directors took turns providing ambulance service at the Fair, especially at the races. The ambulance, along with an attendant was parked in the pit area. The information and this wonderful old ad of the McLaughlin Brothers Ambulance Service was provided by Mary McLaughlin.

Up In the Air at The Missouri State Fair

In 1907 Stroebel's airship was to be a big draw for the Fair. Dick Dallas was the aeronaut or the pilot that was to navigate the air balloon. The first flight was made without incident. The aeronaut believed himself capable of guiding and controlling the machine with ease. Spectators looked in astonishment at the airship while it was making its course high in the air and were more than pleased with the show.

On his second trip, returning from a sail through the air over the city and the downtown districts, the operator of the airship hovered too low over the fairgrounds. As he passed over the racetrack, the rudder struck against the frame work where the aerial trapeze acts were being held. This caused the nose of the giant gas bag to drop against the guide-

Courtesy of Trenton Boyd Collection

Flight so captured the public's imagination that these young people had a souvenir photo snapped. The photo gives the illusion that they had actually flown in a hot air balloon.

line which tore a large hole in it. Mr. Dallas was only a few feet in the air when the airship fell to the track and he escaped injury.

The news account in Tuesday's paper went on to say that every effort would be made to have the balloon back in action the next afternoon. Wednesday's paper reported that Stroebel's airship had been repaired and was ready to make a flight but would not because they had not been able to acquire a sufficient supply of sulphuric acid used to form the hydrogen gas to inflate the air bag. Thursday's paper reported that there wouldn't be a flight that day either because of the high wind velocity and that if it died down he "might" try it late that evening. I could find no account of whether he flew on Friday, the last day of the Fair, or if he called it quits and left town.

The Post Mark on this post card is dated April 7, 1908

Orville and Wilbur Wright had a contract with Fair officials to have one of their aeroplanes on daily flights during the Fair. It was flown at least once around the track and twenty feet in the air. During one performance, their pilot, Clifford Turpin, demonstrating steady nerves and no fear, made a wild dive with the aeroplane over the top of a 45 mile per hour automobile that was making a five mile run (five laps around the track). The aeroplane made a mile in 1 minute and 31 seconds.

The Wright Brothers were trying to raise money and fair goers were craving excitement. They undoubtedly had the pilot perform like that at fair after fair. Such wonders were always billed as educational but entertainment was most definitely the goal.

Ruth Law of Ruth Law's Flying Circus. She was an early day dare devil that appeared at the Fair. Wing walkers and all sorts of aerial acrobatics were part of the biplane shows.

In 1919, Lt. Frank Pickard (Pickard served in World War I) and Miss Franke Homan, both of Kansas City, were married in Pickard's aeroplane at the State Fairgrounds.

A local minister was taken up with the couple, with Pickard flying the plane. After reaching a height of 5,000 feet, Lt. Pickard shut off the engine and the ceremony was performed.

Starting with the World War I era, airshows were very popular and drew large crowds well into the 20's.

Wright Bros. Aeroplane at the Missouri State Fair

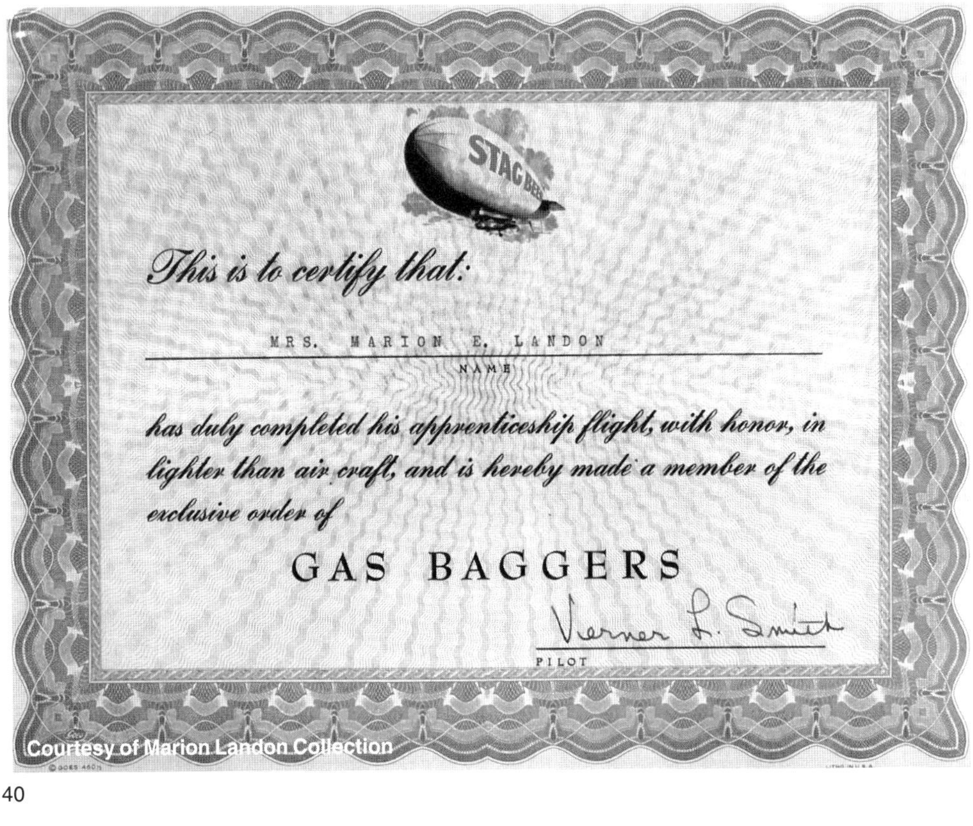

The Griesedieck Western Brewery Company of St. Louis brought the Stag Blimp to Sedalia in 1951. It was in regard to their 100th birthday in the brewery business. Mrs. Marion Landon recalls that her husband, Gene, received an invitation to ride along with a few other couples. It was not really open to the public. It was tethered at the airport and its main mission was to circle the fairgrounds on a certain day and to project messages at night from the lighted billboard on its side. She said the ride was approximately 30 minutes and she remembered being in awe of how quiet it was. One would think that with the big engines there would be noise but it was exceptionally quiet. She said she had no idea when she was riding in it that it was an historical vehicle and had an illustrious history with the military. The Gas Baggers certificate was given as proof that you had been up in the Stag Blimp.

The "Stag" Blimp made an appearance at the 1952 Fair with Werner Smith as its pilot. The blimp was 153 feet long with a diameter of 40 feet. It stood 51 feet high on its landing wheels and was inflated with over 124,000 cubic feet of helium. Mr. Smith explained to Fair officials that the pressure inside an ordinary toy balloon was 22 times greater than the inside of the blimp's envelope. The envelope was new but the gondola or control car had some very interesting history. One of its accomplishments had been to transport last minute supplies to the aircraft carrier Hornet, enabling General Jimmy Doolittle's fliers to successfully complete the now famous first Tokyo Raid.

Mr. Smith explained that the Blimp was powered by two 145 horse power engines mounted on the out riggers which gave it a top speed of 62 miles per hour with a range of 600 miles. The sides of the blimp had over 4,000 small light bulbs and were used to flash the latest news to citizens in the evening.

Dan Patch

Dan Patch Race at the old grand stand in 1909.

Dan Patch, a mahogany bay, Standardbred, was foaled in 1896. He was a direct descendent from Hambletonian 10, who was a direct descendent of Messenger, an English Thoroghbred stallion who was considered to be the progenitor of the trotting horses in the U.S. Four years later, he started serious racing. By 1902, competition was difficult to locate so his owner, Marion Savage, began to race the fantastic speedster against the time clock. In 1905, he paced the mile in 1:55 1/4, a recognized record that stood for 33 years. Dan Patch was the epitome of excellence in this sport. He broke the two minute barrier 35 times in his pacing career. He became a national hero. Products were named after him. There were Dan Patch cigars, coaster wagons, rocking horses, sleds, watches, washing machines, sheet music and even a Dan Patch automobile that sold for $525. Marion Savage purchased Dan Patch for $60,000 in December 1902. He kept Dan Patch's name in the public's eye constantly. Savage owned the International Stock Food Company of Minneapolis, Minnesota. The endorsement of Dan Patch on his products as well as other companies products, exhibition races and barnstorming made Savage millions. On July 11, 1916, while Savage was in the hospital recovering from minor surgery, Dan Patch became violently ill and died of heart trouble. The following day, when his owner heard of his favorite horse's death, Savage took a turn for the worse and died. Their funerals were held on the same day. The entire country mourned Dan Patch's passing. Dan Patch lives on in many ways though. In 1949, *The Great Dan Patch* starring Dennis O'Keefe and Gail Russell was released. Each year Oxford, Indiana holds "Dan Patch Days" to celebrate his life and career. The year end divisional award given by the United States Harness Writers Association to top harness horses has been called the Dan Patch Award. Hoosier Park in Indiana holds the Dan Patch Invitational for the best older pacers in the country. The track is located on Dan Patch Drive. The Minnesota 4-H Horse Association's highest award is named after Dan Patch. In Indiana there is a section of a state road known as the Dan Patch Highway. In the history of harness racing, there are few horses that can compare with the lasting legacy of Dan Patch.

Tomorrow's Race - Will the World's Record Be Broken at the State Fairgrounds?
Dan Patch Against Minor Heir
from the Sedalia Democrat-Sentinel (Sunday, October 3, 1909)

The former is thirteen years old, the but the younger animal will have to travel some to capture the ribbon. Tomorrow afternoon on the State Fair track at Sedalia the people of Missouri will have their first and perhaps their last opportunity to see Dan Patch and Minor Heir, the world's two fastest horses, fight it out for the championship of the world.

Dan Patch is now 13 years old. He has been an undisputed champion for seven years. He is acknowledged everywhere to be the greatest horse of history.

Mr. Hersey, his trainer and driver says that he is ready for a series of miles that have placed him in a class by himself. If Minor Heir beats him on Monday afternoon he will have performed a wonderful feat. State and World records are likely to be broken and horse history made.

The champion will be driven by his veteran trainer, Harry Hersey, while Minor Heir will be piloted by "Bill" Turner, one of the best known and best liked drivers in Missouri. Owner Savage has ordered Hersey to give the pacers every chance and to the let the best horse win. This, with these two drivers, insures a battle royal.

The champions, together with their running pacemakers and several other representatives from the International Stock Food farm, are now enjoying especially prepared quarters on the state fairgrounds, where they will be one of the greatest attractions, at least until after Monday.

This season Dan is defending his titles against the wonderful pacer, Minor Heir, in a series of races arranged by Mr. Savage for the purpose of finding out the respective merits of the two great pacers. So far the horses have appeared only on very bad half-mile tracks, and are just now rounding into pacing form. Their race here tomorrow afternoon will be their second public appearance on a good mile track and great interest naturally centers in that event. Mr. Savage

This was Dan Patch's private railroad car.

will take advantage of this, possibly their last great mile together, and will have a moving picture film made of the race so that a picture, as well as a written history of it may be handed down to posterity.

Records to Stand
"Dan Patch" and "Minor Heir" Did Not Break Theirs Here Today
from the Sedalia Democrat-Sentinel (Monday, October 4, 1909)

The supremacy race for the world's championship honors between Dan Patch (1:55) and Minor Heir (1:59 1/2) was called at 4:25 p.m. today.

Dan Patch was driven by H.C. Hersey, manager for M.W. Savage, Dan's owner, while W.B. Tayor, Sedalia's race horse owner, drove Minor Heir.

The two horses began warming up in preliminary heats at 1:30 o'clcok. The test for the championship honors was a distance of one mile.

Dan Patch covered the mile in 2:07 and a Minor Heir in 2:07 1/4.

It is estimated that nearly 30,000 people witnessed the race.

Courtesy of the Hennepin History Museum

Harold Savage, age 8, drives this sleigh drawn by Dan Patch in 1914. With his good temperament, even children could handle driving him.

Agriculture

Courtesy of the Missouri State Archives

In 1945, the first Fair after WWII, Riley Pankey of Brookfield, MO and his wife drove this 1905 model Sears horseless carriage in the opening day parade. Mr. Pankey was the superintendent of the free display of old motor cars at the fair.

The building behind the horseless carriage is a large "three-in-one" building which housed the Hall of Religion, Agriculture and Horticulture exhibits and Poultry exhibits. In the left wing, chickens, turkeys and ducks were displayed, while the right wing was used for County exhibits as well as farm field crops, country hams, fruits and vegetables, dairy products, including butter and cheese, and a display of bees and honey and apiary equipment. The center section was for all churches that cared to use it and it was usually utilized by one denomination each year.

The fair acquired an Agriculture Building in 1962. The contractor was Tempel Callison Co. It is a one story metal frame building. It houses Missouri's award winning agriculture products such as her famous smoked meats, apiary display and the fast growing Missouri wine produce, along with a variety of foods in the Agri-Missouri market.

Courtesy of the Missouri State Archives

Cheryl Willcockson, of Leeton, MO compares her weight to that of this 69 1/2 pound pumpkin, grown by Frederick Grabau IV of Cole Camp, MO in 1969.

Fine Arts / Floriculture

On the south side of the fairgrounds in a little less hectic area stands two very lovely white wood frame structures. The Fine Arts Building and the Floriculture Building. The Fine Arts Building is a two-story building. When it was first constructed in 1929, the first floor was used for the floriculture displays and the second floor was for art exhibits. The Floriculture Building is somewhat smaller and less elaborate than the Fine Arts Building. It was built circa the 1930's and is suspected of another one of the properties constructed by the WPA crews. As I said before, this is usually a quiet, slower paced spot on the fair grounds. A place to come when you've had enough of the crowds, noise and dust. The floral displays are lovely to the eye and the art work is sometimes startling, sometimes unique but always thought provoking. But every once in awhile this quiet little corner can come up with a few of its own surprises. Such as in 1957, when paintings by two inmates at the Missouri Penitentiary (The Wall) in Jefferson City, MO were awarded blue ribbons in the art competition. The water color was done by Albert Bradford, a life-termer from St. Louis. The oil was painted by S.N. Reese of St. Louis, a holder of two life terms and a 75 year sentence. But that was nothing compared to the furor that raged on the front page of the *Sedalia Democrat* in 1939.

What Makes Art? State Fair Painters Want to Know

The State Fair's controversy on what makes art and what doesn't reached new heights of bitterness last night with some of the less fortunate painters complaining about the judge's decision and one, William A. Knox, of Jefferson City, planning to file a formal protest against the art contest's first prize award to Mrs. Percy Lewis, a 36-year-old Marshall, MO negress.

Meanwhile, Mrs. Lewis is taking the whole argument calmly. Her painting, "Farm Life," was called "the finest example of primitive art I have ever seen" by Austin Faricy, teacher of aesthetics at Stephens College for Women in Columbia, who judged the exhibits. Mrs. Lewis' only remark on the debate was, "They judged it, didn't they."

And while the carefully trained artists, who lost to her unorthodox work, were grumbling and pointing to violations of rules they have learned, fair visitors were crowding to the Fine Arts Building, anxious to see "that painting." She was a little confused Wednesday night by the numbers of people that surrounded her, wanting to know how she painted her picture. "I was certainly surprised when I won it," she said.

On a piece of canvas 3 1/2 by 4 1/2 feet in size, Mrs. Lewis has created a farm and barnyard scene, mostly with oil paint. But in places where she desired to picture a windmill blade, a plow, a pitchfork, or other metal implements, she used aluminum paint that stands out in a strange contrast to the other color materials. Of more startling effect on the crowds, is the fact her drawing is entirely without perspective. Animals roaming happily about the farm yard are approximately the same size. The artist apparently put her easel atop a nearby windmill and painted what she saw looking down. There are only two inches of sky. Explaining the effects she gets, Mrs. Lewis revealed that she

Mrs. Lewis with her husband, Percy Lewis, stand before her controversial award winning painting.

starts her pictures at the top and paints down. She puts the various objects in the picture "just as they come to me." She says she "plants" her pictures.

Mrs. Lewis has been painting since she was six years old. She has never gone to art school, another thing that irritates her rivals, but hopes to someday. She has already received one offer to buy her picture and may sell it, though she painted it "especially" for her husband. Most of Mrs. Lewis' painting is done for Negro ministers, who want symbolic drawings to illustrate their sermons at revival meetings. She also said last night that this is not the first fair prize she has won. In 1933, at the Chicago World's Fair, she entered a hand painted pillow based on the theme of "Suffer little children to come unto me," which won a blue ribbon.

Mrs. Lewis has been married twice, to her present husband for one year. Mr. Lewis is a veterinarian, the only Negro veterinarian, he says, in Missouri.

"Farm Life" by Mrs. Lewis

A sad footnote to this story is that the vehicle of Percy Lewis was struck by a coal truck on Hwy. 24 approximately one year after his wife's triumphant win at the Fair. The impact of the collision threw Dr. Lewis from his auto and the coal truck ran over him. Death was instant. Dr. Lewis was a prominent man in his community and had studied Veterinary Medicine at Manhattan, KS. He was especially interested in sleeping sickness in animals and had been conducting research experiments.

Miss Shirley Kirkpatrick, Assistant Superintendent of the Fine Arts exhibit, is shown with the two prize winning entries from inmates, Bradford and Reese, of the Missouri Penitentary in Jefferson City, MO in 1957.

Poultry & Rabbit

When raising rabbits, it doesn't take long to get double your bunny back. - Marceline Cox (1959 Ladies Home Journal)

Poultry's original home on the fairgrounds in 1903 was the 55' x 122' brick exposition hall that has served as the FFA building for years. In 1905, poultry moved into the 80' x 160' brick building that we recognize as the 4H building. Poultry, a major exhibitor and such a valuable source of income on the farm made a final move to its present location which is now shared with the rabbit exhibitors. The move into the brick building that was originally the manufacturer and machinery diplay took place in the 30's. The structure is 120' x 120' and is a one story brick structure. They also annexed the one story frame building adjacent to them that had been built in the 20's and was known as the Hall of Religion.

In 1911, even our Governor was an exhibitor at the Poultry Building. He won blue ribbon awards with his bronze turkeys. The fair in 1942 was the last fair until the end of World War II in 1945. People were encouraged to have "Victory Gardens" in conjuction with the war effort. Poultry not only provided eggs for the table but aslo meat. Every farm had a laying flock, as did many households in small towns. In 1946, the MO Dept. of Agriculture banned the poultry show for that year. The order was due to the prevalence of Newcastle's Disease which afflicted Poultry.

Noel Hall, a student at the Missouri College of Agriculture, and Ass't. Supt. of Poultry admires this cockerel, owned by Joseph L. Hemmel of Jefferson City in 1942.

The Highway Gardens

The Highway Gardens is a small peaceful park like area. It is a lovely shaded retreat of brick pathways, flowers, rock walls and the lily pond. The rustic archways are covered with vining plants and the picnic tables made of different Missouri woods.

In 1951, T.W. Sayers of Jefferson City, was in charge of the gardens and he told a reporter that he felt that approximately 1,000 people passed through the area every thirty minutes. The reporter did some head calculations and arrived at the conclusion that possibly 20,000 people would enjoy the beauty of the spot on that particular Sunday. As a special service that year the Highway Department was giving away road maps of Missouri.

Mr. Sayers had been an employee of the Highway Department for 31 years and would have been around when E.G. Bylander, Missouri State Fair Secretary, addressed a communique to A.W. Graham on July 10, 1920 requesting

Mrs. Edythe Ross at the organ in the little church.

that he issue an order to road overseers to drag the main traveled highway, prior to the week of August 14. He wanted those roads to the Fair in good shape for the visitors.

In 1955, *The Sedalia Democrat* reported on "The Little Church of Choice" Highway Gardens Show. It stated that the little church was designed on the lines of St. Paul's Episcopal Church in Ironton. There were steps that led to a door and the remainder of the front side of the church was open showing the interior light walls with dark trim and benches for the congregation. On the platform was a church organ which was played most of the week by Mrs. Edythe Ross. Soft music of old favorite hymns would drift out over the peaceful gardens when Mrs. Ross was at the keyboard.

This is the place (stated the article) that weary fair goers love most, a place to sit down awhile on shaded benches and relax, even to take off your shoes and let the soft grass cool burning feet. A place where beauty abounds. Where friends meet and talk and strangers become friends. Keep in mind that we didn't have air conditioned buildings in abundance in 1955. The era of the Highway Gardens is the early 1920's.

Highway Patrol

In 1910, the fairgrounds were policed by Missouri University Cadets. By the early 20's the grounds were patroled by police offers from around the state. Some of them were mounted on horse back. The men furnished their own uniforms. The fair gave them a "star badge", a tent and a cot. They were to bring their own bedding. The pay was $5.00 per day. According to the Sedalia Democrat, in August 1946 the Highway Patrol offices were under the grand stand. By the 1980's, it was disclosed that fairgrounds Highway Patrol Officers numbered up to 80.

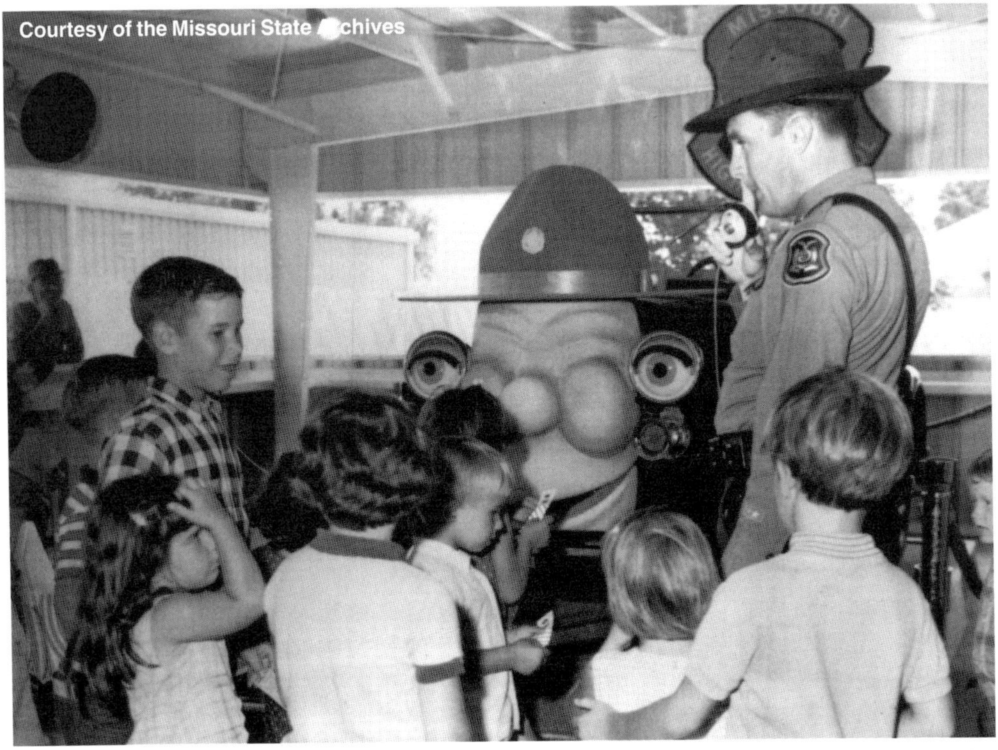
Courtesy of the Missouri State Archives

"Otto the Talking Car" has been a popular attraction for young and old alike at the Missouri State Fair. "Otto" is a 1931 Ford Roadster with animated features. Missouri Highway Patrol Trooper V.L. Reynolds, of Springfield is shown here talking with a group of youngsters and "Otto".

"Otto" in a rare "alone time" moment.

Although Officers say he is old and cranky, he always has some friendly advice for young fair goers on how to stay safe.

Courtesy of the Missouri State Archives

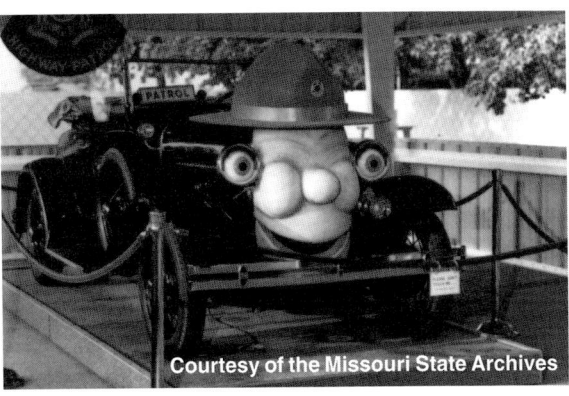

Conservation

1926 was the Conservation's first year on the grounds. They were then known as the Missouri Game and Fish Commission. The first exhibits consisted mainly of mounted displays of fish and wildlife. In 1935, the WPA built the pavilion that with a few modifications is still in use today. The WPA stood for the Works Progress Administration. It was established in 1945 as a massive program to provide jobs for the unemployed. It was part of President Roosevelt's New Deal, a set of initiatives designed to revive the American economy. Between 1935 and 1943, the WPA contructed more than 650,000 miles of streets and highways, 850 airports, 8,000 parks, 120,000 bridges and 125,000 public buildings. Although mainly employing people to perform manual labor, the WPA also established a variety of educational and arts projects such as the Conservation Building at the Fair.

In 1950, the Missouri Conservation had two mobile exhibition units (resembled travel trailers) on the grounds. They were units taken to various fairs throughout the state. Each of the units contained live fish and animal displays.

In 1952, they had many requests for data on farm ponds. There were agents present that pointed out the benefits to both farmer and fisherman to be gained by ponds, contour plowing and soil conservation. Another popular subject was deer season. Specifically, the effect that the 1951 hunting season had had on the herd and the outlook for the future. Another point of interest centered around the Commission's monthly publication, *The Missouri Conservationist*. Patrons could enter their names on a free subscription list at the booth. The magazine at that time was edited by Dan Saults and everyone knew the magazine was in capable hands.

Of course the real excitement at the 1952 fair was the tornado. The fish on display had to be sent back to the hatcheries when the separate water systems became muddy. They were not returned for that fair season and they finished the week with no fish display.

The big attraction at the 1953 event was Woody and the Smoke Eaters and Smokey the Bear. "Woody" was in real life, Herschel Bledsoe, a forestry aide who had organized and led a series of forestry radio programs. Woody and the Smoke Eaters were a hillbilly band that would perform twice per day in front of the Wildlife Building. Smokey was the Forest Service's fire fighting bear. He was animated and delighted children everywhere he went with his deep voice, his songs and messages on wildfires. The plans were that Woody and his Smoke Eaters and Smokey the Bear would appear several times together as well as individual appearances.

In 1951, the casting pool in the rear of the building was added. It was made of concrete and the bottom was painted a deep aqua blue. It was added so that Conservation agents could teach children and adults how to cast. There were casting tournaments held for all ages daily. All contestants used the same equipment furnished by the Missouri Conservation Commission.

Smokey's History

In the 1950's, a bear cub found himself in a forest surrounded by flames. To escape the fire burning around him, he climbed up in a tree. By the time the fire fighters found the scared and hungry cub, the forest was charred and blackened. The fire fighters, park forest rangers and the warden were so moved by the bravery of this little cub that they named him Smokey. They put him on a plane and sent him to the National Zoo in Washington, D.C. to live. Is Smokey Bear that brave bear cub? No one knows but just remember Smokey Bear's message, "Only you can prevent forest fires!"

Missouri Beef House

Courtesy of the Missouri State Archives

The Historic Preservation Office's study says that this building has always served as a dining establishment. They had no record of it ever belonging to the Girl Scouts and Boy Scouts as this picture indicates. Records show it was constructed in 1913. A verbal history that came to me was that the Goodwill Chapel Methodist Church had served food there for years before it became the Missouri Beef House.

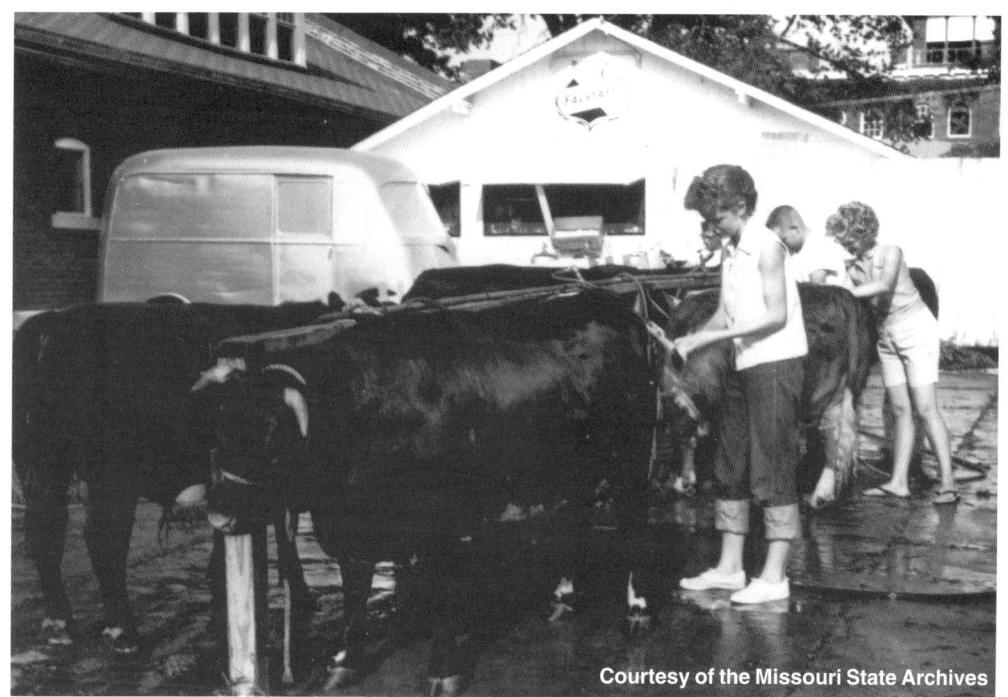
Young exhibitors preparing their animals for the show ring in 1957.

Beef breeds have had notable presence from the earliest days of the Missouri State Fair. The Shorthorn barn was built in 1904. The Hereford Association constructed a barn in 1905. Not to be left behind the Aberdeen/Angus Association had Thomas Bast design them a building which was erected by contractor, Thomas H. Johnson in 1907. All three of the structures were considered as contributing buildings in the historic registar study.

In 1957, the Ralston-Purina Company brought "Champ" to the Missouri State Fair. The giant steer had traveled 22,000 miles and was prepared to spend nine days resting in Sedalia. His proportions were 12 x 19 x 8 feet and Fair visitors were invited to walk through the giant steer's body and see realistic demonstrations of how feed and roughage were made into beef. People entered through doors that opened in the neck. Inside they could see how the vital organs of a steer's body worked in the production of meat. They could also see how a cow made milk and how an unborn calf developed from the first 30 days up to a nine month calf, ready to be born. The exhibit was so life like that the steer's body had the sound of breathing and heart beat. Champ weighed 4,000 lbs. with out his tractor and trailer. His exterior had been built in 29 different parts and leading veterinarians had assisted in making the interior display. Champ hit the road in July of 1956 and in one year had traveled 22,000 miles from the Pacific to the Atlantic coasts. He attended major fairs and livestock shows. They estimated that 650,000 people had walked through Champ's body in an effort to understand the mysteries of cattle production.

Home Economics

The John Deere Building was built in 1909 and was bought by the Fair in 1920 for $2500 from the John Deere Plow Company. It became the Home Economics building in the 1930's.

Home Economics Department - from The Sedalia Democrat (1911)

Wonderful improvement has been noticed this year in the home economics department. More space has been allotted this exhibit and the display is decidedly larger and better. Mrs. Bettie Gentry, in charge of the department, gives it as her opinion that the improvement is due to the instruction given in our grade and high schools on the subject of domestic science. Her statement is verified in the fact that there are such a large number of exhibits by young ladies under the age of 20 years. The young ladies of Missouri especially are taking great interest in this work, their exhibits being of exceedingly high quality.

Not only are the Missouri ladies giving their attention to this part of the show, but ladies from other states are competing. There are exhibitors from Kansas, Nebraska and Louisiana. The exhibit from Louisiana consisted of blackberry jam, which won the premium. The Missouri contributors did not have many berry exhibits, owing to the dry weather in this state. Other fruits and vegetables were more numerous. Fruit cakes are plentiful. They are made and sent to the fair with the hope of winning, and whether they do or not, they are kept for Thanksgiving and Christmas by the makers - the older the better.

Pure Food Exhibit Attracts Many - from The Sedalia Democrat (1911)

The pure food exhibit, under the direction of Dr. W.P. Cutler and his assistants, is attracting a great deal of attention at Art Hall. There is a crowd of ladies around the booth constantly profiting by the demonstrations given, all eager to learn to distinguish the wholesome products from the inferior. The instruction given is indeed valuable to the housewife and those interested in domestic science. It is essential that the head of the household should know how to tell butter from oleo margarine; how to tell whether or not the milk contains a preservative; whether or not the canned goods you purchase from your merchants are fit to eat; if the extracts contain artificial coloring matter and to know many more necessary facts in connection with pure food which are being given out by the pure food and drug commissioner. The lady visitors at the fair should not overlook this exhibit under any circumstances. The men in charge are eager to answer any and all questions.

These events would have been held in the Womens' Building as the Home Economics Building we have today was still the John Deere Equipment Building in 1911.

Courtesy of the Missouri State Archives

The Rocheport Canning Club of Boone County under the leadership of Mamie Alexander entered this display in 1918. Note the glass lids on all the jars.

The Home Economics Building was built by the John Deere Plow Co. in 1909 for display automobiles, buggies, wagons, gasoline engines and farm implements which the company marketed before concentrating on tractors a decade later. The John Deere Building included a two-level office and sleeping room in the center, plus a carriage room, according to the blueprints. The brick foundation was open and covered with wire mesh originally.

When the fair first acquired the structure in the 1920's it was designated as the W.D. Smith Building in honor of the Fair Secretary. During the 1930's it became the Home Economics Building. The architect is believed to be Bast.

Missouri's best cooks and needleworkers carry into the Home Ec Building the fruits of their labors. They come to compete with their neighbors but one competitor in the 1950's was really something. Not only was she 84 years old but she was also blind.

In 1957, Mrs. Ophelia Bowers was named champion of the Missouri Cooks of Yester Year. On the other end of the spectrum were two youthful winners. Richard Weymuth, age 12 of Cole Camp, MO won three blue ribbons out of four entries on his cooking. Sally Allen from Sedalia, won two blue ribbons out of four entries for her sewing. Sally was 13.

Mrs. Bowers, of Sedalia, had been entering and winning since 1951. She had entered sauerkraut, applebutter, two loaves of homemade bread, gingerbread, cornbread and cookies. Everything took a blue ribbon except her cookies and they received a red. She said she was sure that her problem was that she had halved her cookie recipe and it just hadn't turned out right. Mrs. Bowers grew up on a farm south of Stover and raised her family in that area too. She had eleven children. Her son, Enlow, operated the drive-in at 16th & Grand and Pearly, worked for the 7-Up Company. Three of her sons operated grocery stores in Stover, Edmonson and Gravois Mills. Her son Lloyd and his wife Lucille were also operators of one of the Fair's concession stands in the 1940's.

Richard Weymuth said he was just following family tradition as his aunt had won many blue ribbons at the State Fair as well as the Cole Camp Fair. His Grandmother, Hulda Weymuth, had always been a successful contender herself.

Sally Allen had been sewing for two years and came by it naturally as her mother liked to sew and made all the family's clothing. She didn't start on doll clothes as most young girls always did, she had started right out making her own clothing.

Mrs. Bowers and Sally proved that it didn't matter how young or how old, you could still have fun winning blue ribbons at the fair. Richard amply demonstrated that you didn't have to be a female to win blue ribbons with your cooking.

Origins of Fairs and Blue Ribbons

Trade fairs of the 20th Century have perhaps been more in the nature of exhibitions than true fairs in the ancient European tradition. Various industries such as automobile, broadcasting, textile industries or office equipment companies hold annual fairs of their own and often display their ware at state fairs.

In the U.S. the most common type of fair was the county or state agricultural fair. It is believed that fairs in this country originated in the early 1800's when a merchant of Albany, New York organized a rural fair, The Berkshire County Fair at Pittsfield, Massachusetts in 1811 to be exact. He later convinced the New York legislature to appropriate $10,000 a year for six years to provide premiums for agricultural products. Also to recognize products made in homes such as sewing, butter making or jellies and preserves.

In the 19th Century, annual fairs became popular throughout the country. Some of them lasted an entire week. A few of them, such as the Iowa State Fair became nationally famous.

I'm sure most of us have seen the wonderful movie "State Fair". The entire family heads for the fair for a week of fun and competitions. Mama with her mincemeat and papa with his prize pig. And as it always happens on the silver screen, they all go home with a blue ribbon.

The blue ribbon is the most ancient of distinguishing marks of high merit. The color blue was chosen as a symbol of distinction because it was believed that because the sky is blue that it is the highest that man can see.

Ribbons were the traditional badge of an order of knighthood. The Order of the Garter was established by King Edward III in 1348 and is the noble and famous decoration given by the British Crown. Those honored wear broad dark blue ribbons.

Eventually a blue ribbon was used to express outstanding achievements. "Blue ribbon of the turf" is used to describe the famoush English race, the Derby. It is said to have originated with Benjamin Disraeli. It is believed to have been spoken by him when someone accused him of not knowing what the Derby was. To which he replied, "Indeed I do, it is the blue ribbon of the turf."

The blue ribbon tradition holds when it is issued to the liner that is the fastest in crossing the ocean. Therefore, being first in shows and competitions merits a blue ribbon!

Blue Ribbon Medal from 1916 Fair

Photo Courtesy of the Missouri State Archives

Food and Concessions

By August 22, 1901 the Fair Directors were becoming a little concerned with the lack of interest shown in food concessions. To that date there had been no concessions granted for feeding people on the grounds. The Fair's opening date would be September 9. The Directors had at first asked $3,000 for the exclusive privilege, finally dropping it to $1800. But no one showed any interest in investing even at that figure. There was concern that if the crowds materialized that was expected, what would they eat? They again reassured the public that there was good money to be made from serving refreshments.

A short time later one of the colored ministers of the city interviewed Col. Rippey, the Fair Secretary, on the subject. He was anxious to secure space for an eating house. It was also his intention to keep it open day and night. He had surmised that there would be no less than 500 people spending the night on the grounds, tending to the stock, etc. The minister said he would lay the proposition before his congregation and they would act in a few days.

How many concessions they had the first year I do not know but the following year the paper stated. "The ladies of the First Christian Church met last night and decided to erect a frame building, 60 x 20 feet on the main avenue of the State Fairgrounds. The building will be used as a dining hall and the ladies will serve meals during the Fair." This appeared on July 10, 1902.

August 22, 1902, five days into the Fair, the paper reported this development. "The eating accommodations are inadequate and many had to go without dinners. The ladies of The First Christian Church served dinner from 11 o'clock a.m. until about 4 p.m. and there was a line before the front door all day."

In the early days of the Fair no liquor could be sold on grounds. That law had been written into the bill that established the State Fair. To do so was a criminal offense. Mr. T.W. York, the proprietor of Elk Lick Springs, a resort in Saline County, was arrested on the State Fairgrounds on August 19, (the second day of the Fair) for selling liquor. York had paid $25.00 for the privilege of running a lemonade stand. One of the policeman noticed a man walk away from York's stand with a bottle and later take a drink. The matter was reported

Courtesy of the Missouri State Archives

The inside of the concession stand operated by Lloyd and Lucille Bowers. The waitress is Sue Harmon. Note the old beer sign above the ice box. Incidentally that ice box was not there for "atmosphere". It was used.

to Chief of Police, Harry Demuth, who immediately sent a man to the stand to buy one of the bottles. He was unsuccessful, but another man was sent and obtained some liquor. It was put up in a bottle with a formula like a patent medicine and bore the name "Meat and Malt". It was reported to be the vilest poison ever perpetrated on an unsuspecting public. Deputy Revenue Collector, G.H. Pountain, was on the grounds and the man was turned over to him. He was being charged in the United States court.

Reading through the accounts of the old fairs, I was a little amazed at the large numbers of people reported to have been taken to the make shift hospital in the old Administration Building. That is until I found the account from a 1937 paper saying that there would for the first time be inspectors from the Board of Health at the Fair. "The first time in the history of the Missouri State Fair, the State Board of Health has stepped in with two health inspectors in uniforms and taken full charge of the supervision of all eating places at the grounds this year" said Dr. Harry Parker, Commissioner of the State Board of Health, while discussing sanitation at the fairgrounds.

He stated that the health conditions were far better that year than they had ever been. His inspectors were making from two to four calls a day at each stand and were also inspecting the rest rooms and toilets on the grounds. Each person that purchased concession rights on the grounds had been given a letter entitled "General Requirements relative to sanitation of food and drink offered for human consumption."

Prior to the opening of the Fair, Scott Johnson, a State Sanitary Engineer, visited the grounds and made a general inspection of all wash rooms, toilets and rest rooms after which the two inspectors, Teague and Logan, were sent upon the grounds to take charge. John Teauge, Kennet, MO and Hugh Logan, Osceola, MO were the men and they wore white uniforms with black ties and white caps which read Inspector, State Board of Health. They had strict instructions to revoke the rights of any concession holder not living up to the strict rules laid down by the State Board.

Early Concession Stands

There are a few of the earlier concession stands still in operation. They are from the 1930-40 era and are owned by the State Fair. They are typical of those built by the WPA crews. There was typically two aisles with individual entrances. They had benches along a central counter. Some of the first operators of these were Ken and Ruby Williams and Lloyd and Lucille Bowers.

There were no instant foods. An interview with a woman that worked in these stands as a young girl remembered packing water from the Jersey Barns to wash dishes. Real dishes were used, as that was prior to the throw away paper goods of today. Pop and beer was iced down in long metal stock tanks. The men from the cattle and horse barns complained non-stop when the health inspections began. The inspectors required bleach in the ice water that surrounded the pop and beer bottles and the chemical gave the bottles an unpleasant taste. Some of the brands of beer were Country Club and Griesedieck. She recalled that there were 25 chickens butchered every morning to be fried for chicken dinners. All the potatoes had to be peeled. In short, they were truly cooking from scratch.

The Origin of the Corn Dog

Legend has it that two brothers, Carl and Neil Fletcher, were responsible for the first corn dogs. In 1938, the Fletchers were offered a booth at the Texas State Fair in Dallas and needed a product to sell. The brothers had seen a Dallas street vendor selling hot dogs coated in corn meal batter that were baked in molds shaped like ears of corn. This generated the idea to put the hot dogs on sticks, dip them in batter and deep fry them. A much faster process and far more convenient to eat. At this point a legend was born... corn dogs on a stick!

Paying Their Way

On her second engagement at the Fair in 1953, Sally Rand spoke to many of the civic organizations around town. Her talks were centered about how Missourians should support the Fair. She stressed their educational importance but warned not to dismiss the value of the entertainment and especially the concessionaires. She said, "Our part of the Fair is the fun part but without it the prize premiums would not be as large as they are now. It is the shows and concessions which provide 40% of the income which goes a long way to paying for the premiums. In other words 40% of the money taken in by the concessions and shows is "plowed back" into the fair."

In the 1950's there was a Mr. Poindexter that was in charge of concessions and he shared a story about his run in with a would be entrepreneur. Each plot of ground was leased for the Fair and Mr. Poindexter had a map of each place for a concession, the number of feet and just where it was. When he leased a space he colored it red and put the name of the concessionaire on it.

On morning he noticed a man putting up a stand. Mr. Poindexter knew that the spot was leased to a steel company. He questioned the man, "Are you with the steel company?" The man, "No I'm not. I'm putting up a food stand." Poindexter told him, "You can't put it here, this spot is leased." Then the man questioned, "This is State property isn't it?" And Poindexter replied it was. "Well I'm a tax payer and I'm going to put my stand here", retorted the man defending his rights. Mr. Poindexter explained the way the concessions were obtained and why the man could not put his stand there. The man reluctantly tore down the stand.

Mr. Poindexter noted that the "spots" weren't the only thing he regulated. He further explained that meat and supplies were purchased from one company only and that food is inspected by the Division of Health. In that year, 1951, they even had a veterinarian examine the meat to be sure that there was no horse meat being served.

Here is an interesting foot note to the history of the care and feeding of Fair visitors. The building that now serves as a tack shop was built in the 1930's. The structure itself is not important architecturally but it does have a story to tell. It was originally a concession stand operated by and for black Fair visitors. The colored only toilet facilities were down behind this structure. I spoke to many that were of the age to have remembered this, albeit unpleasant, and only a few recalled. I would suppose that Providence in kindness to us, causes us to forget.

Entertainment / Midway

From the beginning, our Fair Directors and Commissioners have always insisted that the Fair was purely educational. Quite possibly all entertainment is education in some way, many times more effective than schools. It slides in the back door and appeals to our emotions rather than to intellect.

The historic study done by the Department of Natural Resources says that the Midway or Carnival area has always been approximately in its present location. It was a portion of the fairgrounds included in the original 160 acre tract that was not immediately developed.

Some form of entertainment area had been set aside by 1903. The Fair Directors, as of July 1, had voted to try to secure an appearance by Ella Ewing for that

Ella Ewing, The Missouri Giantess

Courtesy of Dianne Peck Collection

year's fair. She was quite an attraction in those days as she stood 8 foot and 4 1/2 inches tall and was believed to be the world's tallest woman. The fact that she was a native Missourian would have made her even more appealing. Arranging for her to travel under the primitive conditions of that era, would have been no problem. She had a special railroad car and she could have debarked from her car directly on the grounds. If her appearance ever materialized, I have not found an account.

Ella Ewing, a resident of Northeast Missouri, was the tallest woman in the United States during her lifetime. She was born in Lewis County, Missouri but moved to the community of Gorin, MO when she was quite young. She was a frail child until about nine years of age. But suddenly she started to grow and by the age of 10 she was 6 feet nine inches tall. She was a typical child for her age except that she already towered above the men in the community.

Her parents were hard working farm people with a small income. They tried to make things as comfortable as they could for their daughter, but it seemed impossible to keep up with her growth. In her community she was loved and accepted because her warm personality overshadowed her size. Her parents tried to shield her from the curious, but the task became harder as she grew taller and taller.

At first they refused offers from shows and circuses but finally agreed to let her appear for $250.00 a week plus expenses if both parents accompanied her. Her first out of state appearance was at the Columbian Exposition in Chicago in 1893. There she came to the attention of P.T. Barnum and Bailey Circus. Mr. Ewing was infuriated by their offers but finally consented and Ella was on the road to a livelihood as a side show attraction and the center of attention. She was to have a seventeen year career. She also appeared with Buffalo Bill's Wild West Show and the Sell-Floto Circus. Throughout her pursuit, her mother and father or one of her friends was always with her.

Traveling brought its difficulties because of her size, especially in railroad sleeping cars or carriages. She had difficulties in being comfortable in a home that was adequate for others. Finally over the years she was able financially to not only take care of her parents but built a home that had fifteen foot ceilings, ten foot doors and seven foot windows. Furniture, carriages and traveling accommodations were built to fit her. Finally she did not have to stoop. It has been told that she would have been a few inches taller but she had carried herself, out of necessity, in a stooped position for so long that it became permanent.

She was only forty years old when she died of pneumonia on January 10, 1913. Her burial services were at Harmony Grove church in Knox County. The funeral drew a crowd of an estimated eight to nine hundred people. She had wanted to be cremated as she had always feared grave robbers. Her father could not accept this for his beloved daughter and insisted she have a regular funeral but he intended to safeguard her even after death. An oversized vault that had been a show room display was sunk into the ground, her casket was made in Burlington, Iowa and took the entire force of the Embalming Burial Case Co. working all one night and half the next day to make her final bed. It was designed with fancy octagon ends and was covered with white plush. It took ten men to carry the casket. After it was placed in the vault, they poured cement on the vault before they covered it so that no one could remove the body. Even so, Mr. Ewing kept guard in the cemetery for some time after her burial.

Attractions and Entertainment

The local Humane Society sent a letter to the Fair and to the manager of an attraction on the fairgrounds in 1907. The attraction had a monkey at which soft rubber balls were thrown. The manager was notified that he must cease permitting anyone to throw anything at the animal. The manager up to that time had been doing a thriving business and was making an effort to "adjust the matter" so that he could continue his business of separating the fair visitors from their coins.

By 1909 there was only praise for one J.T. Porter who had "The Hero of the Plains" show at the carnival. He was described as an old newspaper man that had been affili-

Poster advertising for the Midway (circa 1916)

ated with the Kansas City Star and other papers. His shows were described as the best.

As far back as 1799, it has been stated that people thought they must be amused, even if genius, feelings, trust and principles are sacrificed. The Iggorote Village might be an example. In 1909, a Captain A.S. Ash erected what he termed the Iggorote Village that was occupied by twenty primitive Philippines, among them "Chamingo", age 80 years. Supposedly he was the ceremonial chief. This was not an all male group but consisted of women and children also. They were a big attraction. They held shows at special times each day wherein the audience could view them going about their daily lives and an-

Iggorote Village

other feature was that the men held battles, using spears and battle-axes as weapons. I would presume they were acting. Singing of tribal songs, tribal dances and spear throwing was also exhibited. To soothe the public conscience it had been announced that Captain Ash was under a $10,000 bond to insure the safe return of the Iggorotes to their native country.

Col. Casper made an appearance at the 1951 Fair as a ballyhoo man (barker) for the Congress of Freaks. He was very personable and well accepted by the public. He was small in stature (3 foot tall to be precise) but big on charm. It was his fourth appearance at the Missouri State Fair and he was becoming known. Two elderly ladies that always attended the Fair would look him up and bring him cigars. He was 47 years old and had been born in Coney Island, New York. He described himself as a Coney Island hot dog without the mustard! During the war when his show business career lagged he had worked in a defense plant. He had been a valuable asset because he could work in parts of planes that would not accommodate normal sized people. He was with the Cetlin-Wilson Shows.

Other entertainment attractions with Cetlin-Wilson Shows were, 25 Thrilling Rides and 22 Entertaining Shows. Special mention was made of the "Hi Frenchie" Show because its star attraction was Sally Rand. Various other dancers and comedians appeared on the bill with her. The Jerry Jackson Hi Steppers were an all colored musical show. Only colored entertainers were featured. There was an under water ballet called "The Divena Show". This was made popular by the Hollywood "wet" musicals featuring Esther Williams. The performers were in a 500 gallon tank of crystal clear water and were completely submerged through the performances.

There was a motor dome where lions chased motorcycle riders around the walls of the motor dome and then there was the Monkey Circus. That attraction had 40 monkies doing such feats as driving their own little special gasoline powered cars around a 60 foot speedway.

There was a kiddie land with live pony rides, a little merry-go-round, little boat rides, auto rides and the little train. There were the big major rides for the teenagers and adults.

The entire gigantic show had arrived by train onto the fairgrounds. There were 40 double length cars that pulled on to the fairgrounds from their previous engagement in Michigan. This Carnival also played fairs in Indiana, Maryland, Pennsylvania and Virginia. All of this was accomplished by railroad.

A final thought on the carnivals of that more innocent era. Those shows featured Mother Nature's oddities such as Alligator Skin Boy, the Human Monkey Girl, The Fire Eater "Human Electric Dynamo", plus the ever present Sword Swallower. Of course one should never forget the glass house, the snake show, the girl with the green hair and the "Posing Show" with beautiful girls or as we call them, girlie shows. So much of those so called attractions have lost their appeal. We, as a people have been over exposed to everything and so many of the things we use to pay to see are now before us daily. For example, the girl with the green hair. Girls now days paint their hair a multitude of colors and can be seen shopping at Wal-Mart. The Conservation Department has a marvelous snake display free of charge in the pavilion. And as for the "girlie shows" and exotic dancers such as Sally Rand, well let's just say, you can see more exposed on the street today than those girls ever let anyone "peek" at. And Sally did it with so much style. She just had the natural ability to make someone else think that they and she were wonderful.

Sally Rand - The One and Only

To the younger set her name isn't even vaguely familiar and to some it has a slight risque taint, to some it causes raised eyebrows as they describe her as a stripper or a burlesque queen. To others if they studied her career or ever had the privilege of meeting her she was a lady of charm and wit.

Even though she would eventually make an appearance at three separate years of the Missouri State Fair, her first arrival was in doubt for awhile. Headlines blared that

The infamous Sally Rand

Sally was saddened by "No" at the Fair. All of this was only sensationalism by the press as Governor Smith finally settled the matter. In a piece entitled, *"Sally's Fans Still Stirring Up Trouble"* he stated that he had received letters from around Missouri protesting her performance at the Fair. He flatly refused to interfere with Sally's show. The good ladies of Missouri protested her appearance and I have always suspected that they didn't fear Sally's stimulating their men to sin as much as stimulating them to pleasure!

She was living in Chicago when she developed her infamous dance with some shop worn ostrich feathers. She told later that those ostrich feathers made her recall ducks, geese and herons flying when she was a girl in Missouri. She remembered their wings being graceful against the sky. She envisioned a dance that would incorporate their movements. She took the performance to the 1933 Chicago World's Fair and she artfully twirled two seven foot ostrich feathers around her shapely petite figure as she maneuvered to the strains of DeBussy's "Clair de Lune".

She was arrested for indecent exposure but by our standards the performance was tame. Only a few could claim that they had even caught a slight glimpse of her derriere. She was humiliated by the charges and defended herself with, "It wasn't indecent, it was an illusion." And when questioned how

In 1957, Sally's final appearance at the Fair, Jim Hertzer's "Honey Girls" were also on the Midway. Sally was performing in the Cetlin-Wilson's "World on Parade".

she could conceal her nudity she quipped, "The Rand is quicker than the eye."

When she first performed she was paid $125.00 a week, but by the end of summer, in the midst of the Depression, she was raking in $3,000.00 per week. If anyone could be singled out as the salvation of the "failing" Fair in 1933, it would be Sally. She brought the same results to Sedalia in 1951. Our Fair wasn't failing but she did up the gate receipts thirty two percent higher than the previous year.

She was questioned by a reporter if she had always wanted to be a dancer. She admitted that she would have preferred a different path to fame and fortune, but she was young and needed a job. Life had handed her a lemon and she made lemonade. And in her usual optimistic style she flashed that smile and concluded, "I haven't been out of work since I took my pants off."

If her detractors smugly thought she might be tarred and feathered in Sedalia, they were to be greatly disenchanted. Because Sally could charm a dog off a meat wagon. She not only made young men gape but made the babies smile when she attended the Blue Ribbon Baby Show. She was a treasured guest at the first Ham Breakfast as she easily chatted with the dignitaries and their wives. By the end of the week she was flooded with invitations to women's luncheons and swamped with requests to speak at their club meetings.

When she returned in 1953, she had her adopted son, Sean, with her. She had made a whirlwind trip of the state on a publicity tour the month prior to the Fair's actual show time. Again in 1957, she was busy making public appearances for Fair publicity. During the actual Fair she was in great demand and had her picture taken with politicians, beauty queens, babies and every prize winning animal on the grounds.

The one thing that did seem to always upset her was being labeled as a burlesque stripper or an exotic dancer. Her reply was, "The dictionary defines exotic as strange and foreign. I am not strange, I like boys. And I am not foreign, I was born in Hickory County, Missouri!"

Gene Autry

Gene Autry and his horse, Champion, were eagerly awaited at the 1959 Fair. He was even featured on the cover of that year's premium book. He was once encouraged to sing on the radio by Will Rogers when Autry was still a telegraph operator for the railroad. Gene Autry had a set of Cowboy Commandments for all his loyal fans to follow:

He must not take unfair advantage of an enemy.
He must never go back on his word.
He must always tell the truth.
He must be gentle with children, elderly people and animals.
He must not possess racially or religiously intolerant ideas.
He must help people in distress.
He must be a good worker.

He must respect women, parents and his nation's laws.
He must neither drink nor smoke.
He must be a patriot.

All of the silver screen cowboys had commandments or creeds for the members of their fan clubs. Roy Rogers had a club prayer. Only the knights in shining armor could equal the B-Western Cowboy.

Cover of the 1959 Premium Fair Catalog

A Lot of Bull!

In 1951, Seluhm American Boy, a 2600 pound registered bull, owned by Plank & Plank of Gordon City, MO was publicized to be the biggest bull even if he might not be the best. The five year old bull was bred by Paul Selken farms of Smithton, MO and was entered in the Holstein judging. The owners were hopeful that he wasn't only the biggest but also the best. He had quite a successful show record when he arrived at the State Fair. He had taken second place at the American Royal and had done quite well at numerous other fairs that summer.

Getting a bull ready for showing was and is a lot of work. They had to be washed at approximately 4 a.m. that morning to be ready by show time. Extra precautions had to be taken in handling a bull. A wire was attached to a ring in his nose and he was kept moving at all times. No one wanted to give "Boy" a chance to even think about getting angry.

An article pointed out that he was a valuable herd sire but with ground beef selling for 65 cents a pound (keep in mind this is 1951) he was worth a lot of money. In fact, anyway you looked at it, he was a lot of bull!

Maybe those guys needed Toots Griffin to handle their bull. She had been at the fair over thirty years earlier. The picture caption states that Toots Griffin was a champion lady steer rider and the world's smallest cowgirl. "Charlie" the steer was supposed to be the biggest in the world, weighing in at over two ton.

Tornado

Courtesy of Marian Landon Collection

View of the Midway after the Tornado in 1952

Over the years fair goers and exhibitors have been subjected to some really bad storms. In the very early days when the poultry and livestock were housed in temporary structures and tents, a storm created pandemonium by blowing chicken coops about or causing pens to topple and fall. This released horses and cattle that had to be rounded up. And more than one "chicken chase" was conducted on the grounds.

But nothing to date has ever matched the tornado that ripped a path through the grounds at 1:20 a.m. on Thursday, August 21, 1952. It flattened the Cetlin-Wilson Carnival and left one man dead and many injured.

The dead man was Harry Pyle. He, his wife and daughter were in the heavy mobile trailer that was carried 60 feet and dropped. His wife and child were okay but he died of a broken neck. At first it was thought by many that he had drowned as there was a foot of water running in the carnival grounds. His father operated the starting gate for the Grand Circuit Harness Racing and was elsewhere on the grounds when the storm hit.

The Cetlin-Wilson shows sent what was left of two ferris wheels back to the factory for restoration so that they would be in working order for the next fair date in Indiana. Most of their rides sustained damage of some type. But in the short space of 18 hours they were up and running with 70% capacity and the storm debris was removed.

All of the cattle and horses that escaped had been captured. Only one animal died, a prize winning bull owned by Norbert Basten of Wentzville, MO. There were trees uprooted and they had fallen across trucks, cars and food stands. Machinery displays were greatly damaged. Many signs were blown down including the giant overalls that hung on the backside of the grandstand. The Lee's overalls were found and re-hung and everyone had a good laugh trying to surmise what some farmer might have thought had he found them in one of his pastures.

The REA Building was leveled. It represented over a half million dollar loss. It was the newest brick building on the fairgrounds but it might as well have been made of straw. The structure housed 1/6th of the world's largest collection of tropical butterflies and moths. The collection was valued at $500,000 and was a total loss. The building had set just east of the midway entrance.

Lash Larue "King of the Bull Whips" and star of 100 cowboy movies had been appearing in his western show with the Cetlin-Wilson Shows the week the storm hit. He had a little black sports car with steer horns mounted on the hood. The car was not a pretty sight following the tornado.

This had been the Golden Anniversary of the Fair and there were high hopes for increased attendance from previous years but they were disappointed as the numbers had slipped downward a little. Even so, not a bad turn out after such a calamity.

Courtesy of the Missouri State Archives

The tornado uprooted trees and destoryed machinery.

50% Plus 50% Equaled 0%

In compiling this book I have delved through many boxes, not to count the many ancient records and newspapers I have read and how many verbal accounts I have listened to. A great many of the stories I could not document so I dismissed them. But every now and then you hear one of these off the cuff tales that you just have to tell.

In 1952, the Golden Anniversary of the State Fair, a tornado swept through the fairgrounds, killing one man, destroying the newest building on the grounds, uprooting trees and flattening the entire carnival. The next morning, the ferris wheel lay in a twisted mess, greatly resembling a giant pretzel. One can only imagine the fury of the twister that passed through in the dark of night. These people were caught unaware, as they did not have a Civil Defense Warning System like we do today.

Fifty years ago, the concessionaires had a rough go. They didn't have all the precooked and "just heat up" foods that are available today. Pop and beer was iced down in long metal stock tanks and kept covered with tarps. Chickens were butchered and brought in to be fried daily. Potatoes were peeled and dishes were washed. They had never heard of styrofoam. So if you had a food stand, you looked for someone willing to work and someone tough enough to hold up under the drudgery and heat. One particular concessionaire and his wife, John and Mary (I have changed the names of everyone to protect the innocent), hired some sturdy gals that were looking for a little extra money and enjoyed coming to the Fair for party time that took place nightly down in the livestock barns. The Short Horn Cattle and Mule Barn appeared to be the two real "hot spots" after hours in those days.

Among the help was Lou, an old maid that was untouched and intended to stay that way. Her chastity was a garden that she daily weeded and watered, knowing that she wanted no brambles creeping in. Not that she had much to concern her on that score. She had a nondescript shape that you knew had never known silken under garments, only sturdy cotton. Dresses hung like loose sacks from her shoulders, her hair was knotted unattractively at the base of her neck and to describe her face I would have to use a term I heard many eons ago, "a thousand year old seed". And if all that wasn't enough strikes against the poor woman, she had been encumbered with a speech impediment that was bad at any time but rendered her totally devoid of verbalization when distressed. But she could cook and she could take the heat of the kitchen on the hot August afternoons in the pre-air conditioned days.

When the food stand closed about 10 o'clock the other girls did a light "toilet" and hurried down to the mule barn for a little fun before turning in when the night became cooler. Everyone that worked there had a cot which they would set up outside the concession stand and sleep under the stars so as to catch whatever breeze might exist. But not Lou, she wore a long white heavy cotton gown with full length sleeves and a gathered white sleep cap for her head. Her cot was always inside the confines of the food stand with the doors firmly latched from the inside. Just in case any of those whiskey drinkers from the mule barn had any ideas. John permitted this as she was his sister and he understood her odd ways, and he knew that Mary had to have Lou's help to keep the food prepared.

John and Mary were in their cots under the stars, along with their other employees and Lou was secured inside the stand when the twister hit at about 1:20 a.m. Not only were things banging and flying through the air but trees made terrible sounds as they were ripped from their spots. And the rain came down in buckets! Within minutes water was flowing everywhere and terror filled Lou's heart. She must find her brother John. He would protect her. Out into the awful night she dashed, but nowhere was John or Mary to be found. They and everyone else had made mad dashes for the horse barns and hopefully safety. For some unknown reason, Lou ran wildly into the mule barn, screaming like a banshee. The fear had rendered her speechless.

And for some reason known only to them, all those mule men slept barefoot up to their chins and were in the process of trying to find their britches when Lou came racing through the barn. The sights she saw set her to screaming even louder as she whirled to face the tornado rather than the spectacle she had just witnessed. As she dashed out she lost her footing and rolled in mud and muck. It was not a pretty sight when John and Mary found her. When the sun came up the next morning, she flatly refused to come back to cook. Her reasoning being that "all those mule men know I saw them!" So John and Mary devised a scheme where the mule men in rather loud voices discussed who that white figure could possibly have been in the barn during the storm. "It sure was a puzzlement to them," they said. Finally convinced that her honor was still intact she came back to the kitchen, much to Mary's relief.

Poor Lou, those mule men were so indifferent to her as a woman that she had nothing to fret about. I heard once that sex appeal is 50% what you've got and 50% what people think you have. In Lou's case, 50% plus 50% equaled zero!

Machinery Building, State Fair, Sedalia, Mo.

Courtesy of Trenton Boyd Collection

This building was built in 1909. Awnings were added at fair time and it was used as the Machinery Building. The Poultry and Rabbit Building moved into this building sometime in the 30's.

Courtesy of the Missouri State Archives

This Ferguson Tractor display was in 1947, not long after World War II. Many older farmers still used horse power but the tractor was coming on fast.

Machinery has apparently been displayed in the present day location since the 1920's. The exhibition area is crossed by four asphalt surfaced east-west roads. Demonstration buildings are now a part of this portion of the fairgrounds.

University Building / FFA

The University Building structure is one of the three oldest on the fairgrounds. It was built in 1903 for $10,672.00.

The old University Building (FFA Building) was built in 1903 for Poultry. In the 1920's it became the building for educational exhibits from the University of Missouri and 4H Clubs, as well as the latest scientific findings at the State Experiment Station. Industrious 4H Youths assembled displays of clothing, canned foods, art work and wood work. In the early 50's they moved into what had been the Missouri Building.

Scott Sitner, Ridgeway,MO; Sharon Munholland, Kansas City, MO; Billie Lawrence, Kansas City, MO and James Hermording, Sweet Springs, MO inspect a milkcan cart made by Edward Friedrich, Harrisonville (circa 1950's).

FFA Motto: Learning to Do, Doing to Learn, Earning to Live, Living to Serve. There are 457,278 FFA members in the 50 states as well as Puerto Rico and the Virgin Islands. The FFA operates on local, state and national levels.

The FFA time line is as follows: **1917** - Smith-Hughes act establishes Vocational Agricultural courses. **1920** - Henry Groseclose, an Ag teacher in Blackburg, VA organizes Future Farmers of Virginia. Soon similar groups are established across the country. **1926** - New Farmers of America (NFA) was formed in Virginia for African American boys interested in agriculture. Their first convention was in 1935. That same year the American Royal Livestock Show invites Vo-Ag students to participate in Kansas City, MO. **1928** - At the American Royal, 33 students from 18 states establish Future Farmers of America. Dues were 10 cents annually. The annual convention was held in Kansas City from 1928 - 1998. **1929** - The official colors, National Blue and Corn Gold, were adopted and still used today. **1933** - Fredrickstown, Ohio FFA members arrive at National Convention in crisp blue corduroy jackets with the FFA emblem on the back. Delegates adopt the jacket as official dress. They are still worn today. 50,000 are manufactured yearly. **1948** - FFA Week is celebrated during George Washington's birthday to recognize his pioneering contribution to American agriculture. **1953** - FFA celebrated their silver anniversary. President Eisenhower addressed the FFA Convention. He was the first president to speak to the FFA. Since then speeches have been made by Presidents Gerald Ford, Jimmy Carter, George Bush and Ronald Reagan. **1965** - The NFA organization merges with the FFA and gains 50,000 members. **1994** - Corey Flournoy is elected National FFA President, becoming the first African American FFA President.

The FFA continues to expand opportunities for agricultural career preparation. Their move into their new facilities here in 2002 will leave the old University Building free to become the Missouri Frontier Building. Its mission is to show how the West was born here in Missouri. A Lewis and Clark keelboat, a conestoga wagon, a Butterfield stagecoach and demonstrations of primitive skills are just of few of the attractions.

Missouri Building / 4H

For about 20 years (during the 30's&50's), the Missouri Building was the permanent home of World's Fair Exhibits. The building was dedicated August 14, 1935. Displays used at the New York, San Francisco and Chicago Expos were re-exhibited there, depicting the state's natural resources, industries and historic background. There were replicas of Arrow Rock Tavern, the first Missouri home built by Gen. Jean Baptiste Valee in St. Genevieve, MO in 1782, and a pioneer cabin from the Shepherd of the Hills country in Taney County.

An article about the cabin appeared in the West Plains newspaper on September 9, 1932. *An Ozark cabin exhibit at the Missouri State Fair attracted attention and is considered one of the most interesting displays. The cabin was dismantled at the Bookout Place near Mooric Ferry in Taney Count and*

Poultry Building, State Fair Grounds, Sedalia, Mo.

Courtesy of Trenton Boyd Collection

This building was built in 1905 as a Poultry Building. It was the Missouri Building until the mid 1930's when it became the present day 4H Building.

the pieces moved to Sedalia where they were reassembled in original form in Ozark scenic surroundings and a water fall also was duplicated with rocks and materials taken from Taney County. The cabin was furnished with antique furniture and fixtures from the School of the Ozarks museum near Hollister. The exhibit attracted favorable comment and attention.

Courtesy of the Missouri State Archives

Interior of the Missouri Building

I was six years old when I attended my first fair in 1949. I have three memories of the day. Eating fried chicken (brought from home by Mother) on a blanket beside our car. Temporarily losing sight of my Father in the Midway and being scared that they had lost me. And, the Missouri Building. The inside was cool with water running beside the reconstructed log cabin and there was an old mill wheel turning. I recall standing on a little foot bridge and marvelling at the beauty of it all.

Greg Grupe, of Smithton, MO, displays his blue ribbon collection of insects for his 4H project.

4H is a non-formal educational program for youth. The person in charge at the local level is the Extention Agent. Funding for 4H is provided by the U.S. Department of Agriculture, the State University and County Commissions.

The "H's" stand for Head, Heart, Hands and Health. The 4H Pledge reads: *My HEAD to clearer thinking, my HEART to greater loyalty, My HANDS to larger service, My HEALTH to better living.* Members learn by doing, such as cooking, raising animals, environment, computers and leadership. In 2000, there were 6,834,338 young people in membership, 52% were girls and 48% boys.

Sheep & Goat Pavilion

Early in 1955 the legislature appropriated $100,000 for a new sheep and goat barn. By August, the framework was up with the showing section in the center complete. Many items, such as pens, were temporary, to be completed in 1956. The building was erected by Dalton Coal Co. of Columbia, MO.

The new sheep and goat pavillion was a far cry from the 1906 fair. There was a great sheep show in 1906, without even one Missouri sheep in it! The Missouri Sheep Breeders Association avowed to place the sheep show on the map, so to speak. And so they did, the fairgrounds is now the off season host to the Ram and Sheep show attended by persons from all over the United States. As well as a stunning exhibition and show during the fair.

Identical Habits?

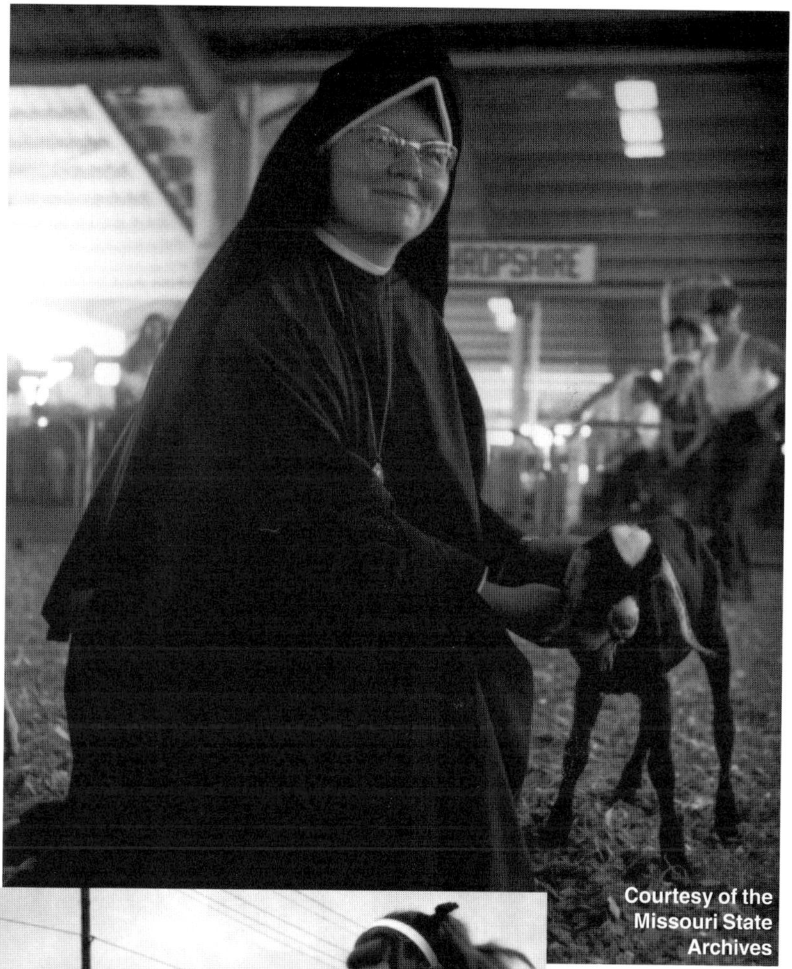
ROPSHIRE
Courtesy of the Missouri State Archives

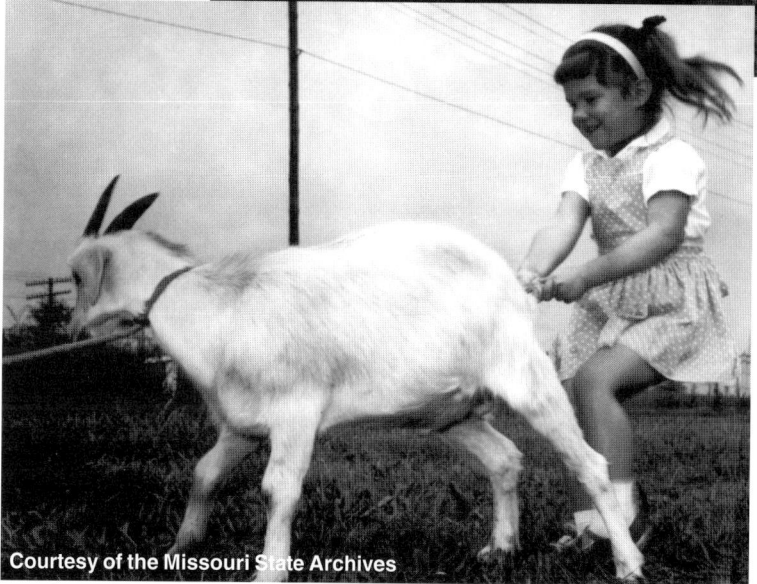

High Fashion: All dressed up with nowhere to go. (1969)

Courtesy of the Missouri State Archives

An animal and child at play. *"It is the sweet, simple things of life which are the real ones after all."* - Laura Ingalls Wilder (1942)

Sheep & Swine

Sheep and Swine Building, State Fair, Sedalia, Mo.

Photo Courtesy of Trenton Boyd Collection

Paralleling the Coliseum's interest to farmers is the Swine and Sheep pavilion, "Porker's Palace and Exhibition Hall for the Golden Hoof," which is used for sheep shows, hog competition and hog auctions. The massive brick, tile, steel and concrete measures 276 by 284 feet and was built in 1922 at a cost of $135,000.

Courtesy of the Missouri State Archives

Can you make a silk purse from a sow's ear? Sally Rand is pictured here in her Christian Dior gown, diamond necklace, earrings and tiara. Sally generously loaned a pair of her diamond earrings and tiara to the Grand Champion sow, owned by A.H. Meyers & Son of Kansas City, MO. Always, a good sport, this was 1957 and Sally's third and final appearance at the Missouri State Fair.

White City Campground

As described by the historic study of 1991. The old White City Campground is a rectangular strip of gently rolling land between the mile race track and the eastern boundary of the fairgrounds (U.S. Rt. 65/South Limit Avenue). If you look at the 1937 map on page 10 you can see where this camp ground used to be.

Here visitors once camped for free as early as 1907, when additional acreage was purchased for the purpose. Many visitors camped in tents which could be rented for a nominal fee, while others brought their own. Fuel for cooking, shower baths and cold drinking water were provided free of charge.

A press release around 1920 stated that about 3,000 people had camped in White City the previous Fair year. It went on to say, "They brought tents and camping equipment with them or rented those on the grounds for reasonable prices. They lived in cool, shady nooks away from the noise of the crowds yet within ten minutes walk of any part of the fairgrounds. They had electric lights, ice water, grocery store, a meat market, a community ice chest, cafe and cafeterias at hand where meals or provisions could be procured cheaply. So economically did they live that it was found a family could live as cheaply there as at home. So spend Fair Week as a citizen of White City."

Today this is primarily a parking and picnic area.

Ham Breakfast - The Fair's Biggest Social Event

This admittance ticket made for the 1971 Governor's Ham Breakfast was made to be kept as a souvenir in celebration of our 150th year of Statehood. Phyllis Diller was a guest that year and autographed this ticket. Other souvenirs given out that year were lapel pins in the shape of the state.

The biggest social event of the 1951 Missouri State Fair or any of the other annual expositions here, was the old fashioned country cured ham breakfast that was held on a Wednesday morning of Fair Week. John Snyder, Secretary of the Treasury of the United States, a former Sedalian and a native Missourian, was the speaker for the event which was attended by dignitaries of both political parties as well as from agriculture, business and industry of the state.

Arrangements for the big event were made by Robert E. Lee of Columbia, MO. He had secured the members of the Quisenberry Extension Club to prepare and serve the breakfast in the "Hi Frenchie" tent in the carnival grounds. This was the tent Miss Sally Rand was appearing in. This was Miss Rand's first appearance at the fair, which was the subject of much controversy.

The breakfast went off without a hitch and many high officials were in attendance. The large tent in the midway of the Cetlin-Wilson Shows had a large table placed on the stage for the honored guests. Newspaper men and other honored guests were at a table directly in front of the stage. Then several long tables running length wise in the tent to took care of the many visitors.

There was an invocation by Rev. Baxter Walters of Liberty, MO and then Robert E. Lee and the toast master kept the audience laughing during part of the breakfast. During the ceremonies the stage dropped about two inches and although it appeared to be serious at first, it ended up being a joke about all the heavy "hams" setting on it.

Carl Tising of High Point, MO took the Champion and Reserve Champion Ham awards. He competed with over 60 hams for the honor. A competitor noted that the Tisings had been champions "too many times to recall". The Tising Family had shown hams for more than thirty years and a lovely silver tray was presented to the family by Senator Hennings.

Governor Smith was called upon to make a few remarks and he praised Fair Secretary Bill Preston for the biggest ham breakfast ever served anywhere. And he called attention to the crowds at the Fair that kept getting bigger and better every year.

Then Mr. Hill arose and read several telegrams from Virginians making friendly attacks on Missouri Hams and defending their Smithville VA Hams. Following this Mr. Hill introduced Secretary Snyder. His remarks are as follows.

"It is a real treat for me to join with fellow Missourians here at the Missouri State Fair and partake of the old fashioned hospitality which has always characterized Missouri people. Good food and plenty of it has long been a noted ingredient of the Missouri hospitality. Typical of its many fine breakfast dishes would be its ham and biscuits. And I am glad to give credit where credit is due; to the gifted Missouri ladies who prepared the ham and all its trimmings for this sumptuous breakfast. The entire fair is of course, a fine tribute to the talents and skills of Missourians. I am happy to be here this year and share with you the pride that is all Missouri's, in this exposition of the many diversified products of its farms and factories. This annual State Fair at Sedalia has been most appropriately named "The show window of the commonwealth". It is truly an

inspiring display of agricultural and industrial achievements which have steadily added so much to the sound growth and progress of our state."

He spoke of the resources of the state and continued with, "While the frontiersmen were willing to share their hit and miss experiences with fellow pioneers, the lack of communication facilities and the dearth of scientific guidance in the choice and management of land and in the better breeding of livestock brought many disappointments and many failures. As a result farming in the 19th century progressed slowly. Farm mechanization, it is true, has shown considerable advancement by the close of the century. But the mechanical improvements did little to make farm home life less tedious and more interesting. The farm women were still plodding along at back breaking tasks. About the only thing that made life more interesting for them prior to 1900 was the party line telephone. There was no other electrical equipment of any kind in farm homes except an occasional incandescent light in favored spots, near the towns. A rotary egg beater or a kitchen sink provided enough of a novelty to cause excited comments.

It seems almost inconceivable to us of the present mid-century generation, who take for granted the many inconveniences of farm and home life and all aspects of modern living, that such conveniences were not only unheard of but undreamed of as little as 50 years ago. Today we can travel to this great exposition from vast distances in a matter of hours by plane, or high powered automobiles. Yet back in 1901, when the Missouri Fair was first inaugurated, it took a full day for families to come by buggy or wagon from as short a distance as

The famous auctioneer, Leroy Van Dyke, at the Ham Breakfast (circa 1957).

25 miles. Yet many came - and came from great distances despite the hardships of travel. And we owe much to them for their foresight and vision in the establishment an important role in disseminating information and inspiration for the greater productivity of agriculture and industry. Tractors have replaced horses. Trucks and automobiles have replaced wagons and buggies. New and better breeds of livestock replaced less profitable ones. Improved methods of marketing and processing have brought the many diversified products of this state into world markets. All this is twentieth century progress!"

The breakfast became a tradition and in 1952, the Golden Anniversary celebration of the fair itself saw 350 in attendance. Governor Smith was the main speaker and Hugh Alewel of Concordia had the Grand Champion Ham. It was auctioned off and brought $220.00. It was purchased by Eugene Preston of the Liberty Tribune for a group of people who sent the ham to Adlai Stevenson, Democratic candidate for President.

The Governor on a light note suggested that there be a law enacted that compelled packing houses to cure hams by the old fashioned country method.

The Third Annual Ham Breakfast had choice country cured hams from 19 different ham producers in 16 counties. A few of those furnishing hams were Morris Burger, California; Morris Tuttle, Prairie Home; L.E. Baischter, Columbia; W.H. Gardner, Rocheport; Hugo Alewel, Concordia; Loyd Tising, High Point; L.E. Sybert, California; and Jim Klinefeller, Columbia.

Bob Hill, the Ambassador for country cured ham was the toastmaster and a queen was chosen and crowned Miss Country Cured Ham. An added attraction that year was the hog calling contest. The three participants were Cordell

Governor's Ham Breakfast 1984. Pictured with Governor Bond and his wife Caroline is Gene Landon, long time restauranteer and caterer. Mr. Landon owned The State Fair Restaurant located in the State Fair Shopping Center. The restaurant walls were covered with Fair memorabilia.

Tindle, the Associate Editor of the *Missouri Ruralist*, who came from a long line of hog callers, N.L. Farmer from Polo, who had shown hogs at the Missouri State Fair longer than any other breeder and Morton Tuttle from Prairie Home, the most publicized producer of country hams. Tuttle claimed he produced the finest country hams in the world. The toast master cautioned that the hog calling was not to be confused with calling the guests to breakfast.

The Smith-Cotton Cafeteria was the setting for the 1955 Ham Breakfast and the guest speaker was Missouri's own Harry Truman. 600 guests heard the former President speak and then observed as he awarded the Grand Champion ham trophy to Morris Burger of California, MO. Morris Burger was a 20 year old agriculture engineering student and beat out many of his family members for the award. Defeated family members included his father, sister and three other relatives.

600 pounds of ham were donated by five producers. They were the Tisings of High Point, the Burgers of California, Bud Gardner of Boone County, Alewels of Concordia and Tuttle. The hams were brought to the Pacific Cafe on Main Street to be sliced by Dutch Kirchofer and Warren Poindexter. Mrs. Norman Scotten, manager of the school cafeteria, oversaw the preparation of the food. The hams were auctioned by Olen Downs and Jesse Paul with the Grand Champion Ham bringing a record breaking $840.00.

Closing comments were made by Bob Hill, the toast master. "I've attended many ham breakfasts, but this was the largest and most spirited one I've ever attended." Was he trying to say that they just kept getting bigger and better?

In 1957, the site for the breakfast was again in the Smith-Cotton Cafeteria. The basketball coach for MU, Sparky Stalcup, was the toast master with the University's popular football coach, Frank Broyles, giving a short talk. Governor Blair had finalized his plans to be on hand and the ham was to be prepared and served with red eye gravy, eggs, fried potatoes, hot biscuits and Missouri honey.

Several years later saw Gene Landon serving the breakfast in various locations. One being the new shelter house at the camp grounds. W.C. Askew, the Fair Director, wanted to "initiate the place". One shared memory of that breakfast was a person that recalled Loyce Askew, the Director's wife, dancing to Lawrence Welk music during the breakfast. Gene served the breakfast in the old stand by tent in 1974, following the now infamous Ozark Music Festival.

Other caterers for the event over the years have been Colie Ervin (he also served as a Fair Director), Maxine Griggs, and Katy Williams of Encore Catering. The event was held in the Mathewson Exhibition Center in 1995. Conflicts with other scheduled events made that a very unworkable plan and it was moved back to the tent just north of the Fair Director's residence. Somehow that tent seems so appropriate. Perhaps it's nostalgia about the very first ham breakfast being served in infamous fan dancer, Sally Rand's tent, on the midway. After all she was a born and bred Missouri girl from Hickory County, where most folks had a smoke house!

Other Interesting Facts & Information

Health Issues

About 1950, the Pettis County Chapter of the National Foundation for Infantile Paralysis (Polio) in cooperation with the state organization decided to sponsor a booth at the State Fair that year. A state representative of the organization was arriving in Sedalia to help prepare the booth and make arrangements to distribute literature on Polio while the booth was open.

Harold Barrick and Mrs. Emmet Sullivan were to be in charge of the booth and along with other volunteers would be on hand to give out information on infantile paralysis. The display was located in the Educational Building and consisted of numerous pamphlets and an Iron Lung exhibit. The Iron Lung was a common name for an apparatus for producing respiration by rhythmically altering air pressure applied against the chest walls of a person who cannot breath normally. Which was the case of many attacked by Infantile Paralysis. Unfortunately some people were dependant on an Iron Lung for many years.

Polio was every mother's nightmare. In 1952, Jonas Salk used his Polio Vaccine on volunteers. The volunteers happened to be his wife, three sons and himself. The vaccine proved to be successful and the dreaded crippling disease was finally controlled. Prior to that it struck viciously, usually to children between the ages of five and ten but was no respecter of age. President Roosevelt was stricken at the age of 39. Although it placed him in a wheel chair, he still managed to campaign and win the Presidency three successive times.

Armed Forces Day

From the era of World War I right through World War II, the military and our service men have received recognition and a spot on the fairgrounds.

This State Fair poster from 1918, advertises quite prominently that the Army and Navy Display covered 14,000 square feet of space.

The Fair was not held in 1943-1944 because of World War II and even though it resumed in 1945, it was rather low key. The front page coverage in 1946, announced the Fair as the first major post-war Missouri State Fair. One of the events mentioned was exhibits by the United States Army Caravan, including a demonstration of close formation flying by Army Air Force planes over the fairgrounds.

Listed also was a full exhibit by the United States Army Air Corps with the latest in Air Force equipment. The special attraction was to be a mass army induction. One young man from each county in Missouri was to be inducted at an early afternoon service in front of the Army display.

The paper announced in 1951, that the World War II trophies were on display. It said the French Friendship Train Box Car which had been cleaned

Advertisement for the 1918 Fair.

and repainted would have in one end war trophies from the European and Asiatic theaters of World War II. The other end was to have posters telling of the American Legion.

It was sponsored by the 40 and 8 Society and The American Legion. Outstanding work had been done by Jake Venable who had repainted all of the plaques. The small French built box car in no doubt was the oldest "structure" on the fairgrounds. And it had been designed to haul cattle. But during both World Wars this and similar box cars were used in France to transport troops (40) or horses (8).

After World War II, the French National Railroad donated one of the box cars - filled with gifts from the French people in response to an American grass roots war relief effort organized by columnist, Drew Pearson, to each state. Local members of Voiture 333 of the 40 & 8 Society, a group that exists within the American Legion, clean and decorate the car each summer. It sets under a gable roof supported by slim metal posts set in concrete next the Home Economics Building.

Courtesy of the Missouri State Archives

The Big Boys

Everyone is familiar with the Budweiser Clydesdales, but few of us have known how extensively the giant six horse hitches have been used in promoting business over the years.

In 1911, with President Taft looking on, Boone Yoder, a master of six in hand put the huge six horse team of Percherons through their paces. The crowd applauded at the maneuvers of the big horses as they wound, unwound and galloped away in front of the grandstand. They were owned by Lafayette Stock Farm of Lafayette, Indiana. They had been brought to the Missouri State Fair to show Missourians what magnificent animals the company owned. The company had twelve stallions on exhibit in the heavy horse barn and the six horse hitch was installed in a special tent just west of the coliseum.

In addition, over the years, other companies have used the gentle giants to promote themselves. Swift & Co. had a lovely matched six horse hitch of iron gray Percherons. The Wilson & Co. Meat Packers of Chicago had a six horse hitch of Clydesdales in 1953. Also in 1953, the Budweiser Beer Co. brought a miniature brewery wagon that was pulled in perfect cadence with an eight white mule hitch. On a trip out West, August Busch had seen the mule hitch and felt it was the perfect promotional tool to send around to various fairs.

There was a mammoth sextet of perfectly matched Clydesdales at the fair in 1932. No they weren't Budweiser's. They were owned by the Chicago Stock Yards and they were touted as being used for heavy short hauls about the pens of the world's largest live stockyard. They were featured that entire week on the evening horse show program. Their job was to dazzle and demonstrate that the race horse wasn't the only equine family member capable of spectacular and flashy acting.

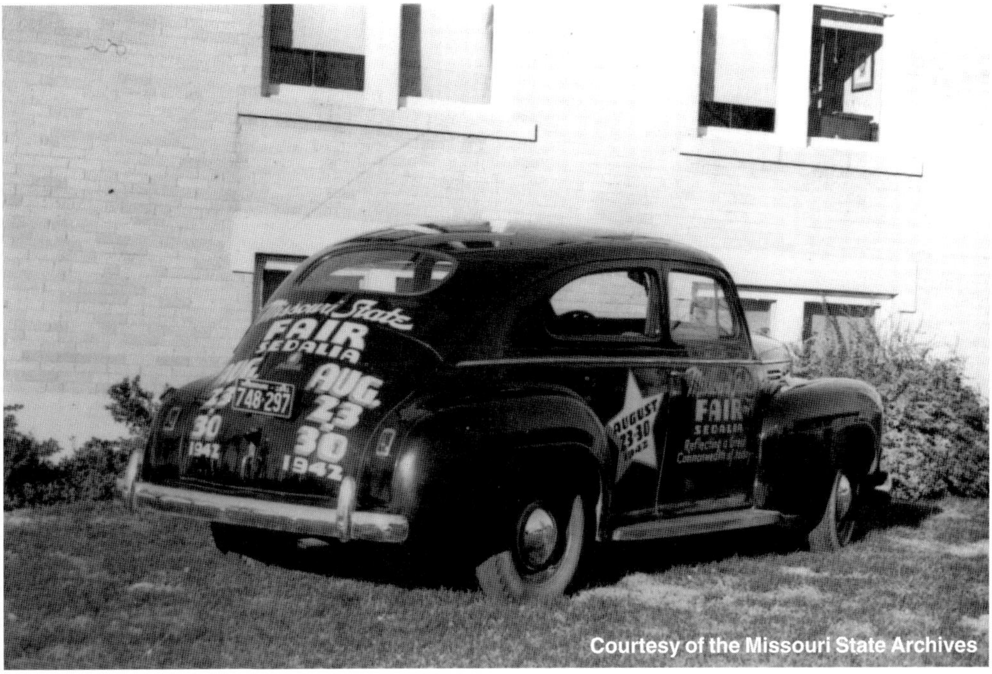
FAIR
SEDALIA
AUG
23
30
1942
Courtesy of the Missouri State Archives

This car was used in 1942, the last fair until after World War II.

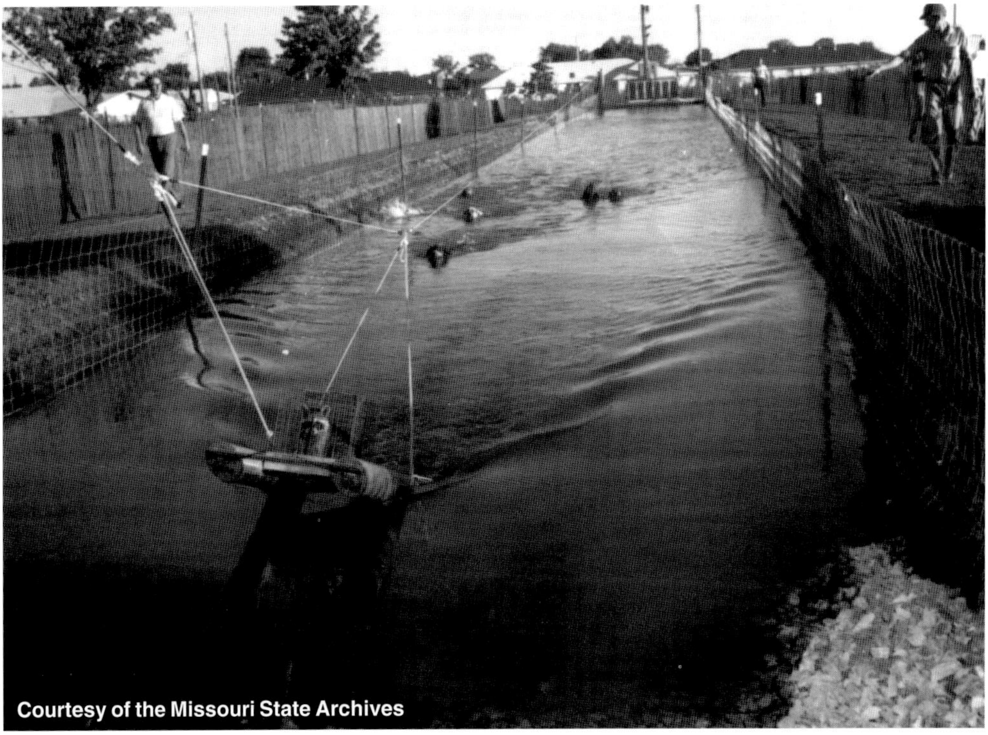
Courtesy of the Missouri State Archives

The sport of Coon Hunting and fine Coon dogs is still alive and well as indicated by the water races.

Draft Horse Pull

Carl Day of Koshkenong and his team pulled a 230 percent load to take first place at the 1957 Missouri State Fair.

Over the years the draft horse pull was held in various locations around the grounds. It has now been placed inside the Coliseum. Call it nostalgia, but the event appears to gain new fans and interest each year. The horses are hitched up to a sled, which is piled with sacks of concrete to determine the percentage pulled of their own weight. Besides being an entertaining feature full of suspense and masterful skill, the team pulling event gives the Missouri horseman a chance to judge and observe the breeds which are more suitably adapted to hard labor.

Shuttle Buses

From the Sedalia Democrat August 17, 1952 - *Persons who usually have tired feet after tramping around the 276-acre State Fairgrounds will get a "break" at this year's golden anniversary Missouri State Fair. Especially con-*

structed shuttle buses will be pulled around the main part of the fairgrounds by farm tractors, providing fair visitors a comfortable method of travel to various points on the grounds. Each bus will seat 24 passengers in such a manner that they will be able to look out over the heads of the crowds. It will be possible for a sightseer to ride until he sees something of special interest, then get off for a closer look. As all buses will travel the same route, he can catch a later bus and complete the trip around the grounds.

Float on South Ohio Street in the opening day parade for the 1957 Missouri State Fair.

Beauty and the Beast

Miss Cynthia Ruth Kueck, 1974 Missouri State Fair Queen, is pictured here with Betty, a four year old jenny owned by Chipman and Kohl of Perry, MO. The mule was the World Grand Champion for the second consecutive year in 1974.

It wouldn't be a Fair without high school marching bands! Pictured here is the Lincoln High School Marching Band in 1957. **1st Row:** Pauline Christian, Sue McCullen, Kay Christian, Edgel Christian, Linda Kroenke, Marlene Meyer **2nd Row:** Mrs. Dorothy Brody, Elroy Kroenke, Sharon Swingler, Weldon Brody, Lawrence Reine, unknown, Janice Berry, Lois Eken, Charles Dundas, Leroy Davis, Jimmy Mahnken **Third Row:** Edith Ann Sartin, unknown, Iva Mae Kriesel, Kay Owens, Bonnie Fischer, unknown, Eleanor Berry, Dorothy Johnson, Robin Suhl, Janice Hansen **Fourth Row:** Darrel Dundas, unknown, Cynthia Delozier, Virginia Mueller, Velda Eckhoff, Jerry Wischmeier, Bud Carney, Charles Keseman, unknown, unknown **Fifth Row:** Wayne Attwood, Ralph Kreissler, Fred Wenig, Larry Meyer, Willard Reine, Carol Carney, Dixie Owens, unknown, unknown.

A special thanks to Pauline Keseman Rambow, Lois Eken Harms and Bonnie Eken Gensler for identifying those in this picture.

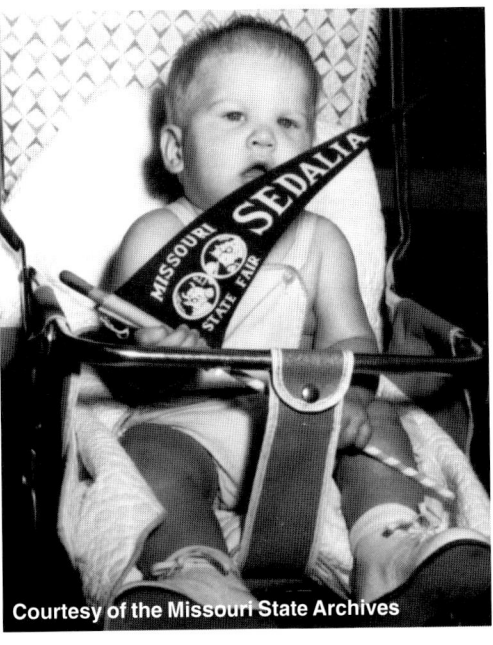

State Fair Fan
Young and old always enjoy the fair! (circa 1965)

Garry, Barry and Larry Yack of Excelsior Springs, MO are presented a plaque by Myrna Lee Miller, of Sedalia. The three young "moonshiners" were winners of the novelty classification in the opening day parade at the 1957 Missouri State Fair.

Lots of kids lined up for the free hats and balloons the MFA handed out (circa 1950's)

Fair Advertising & Post Cards

A collection of patriotic post cards from 1918.

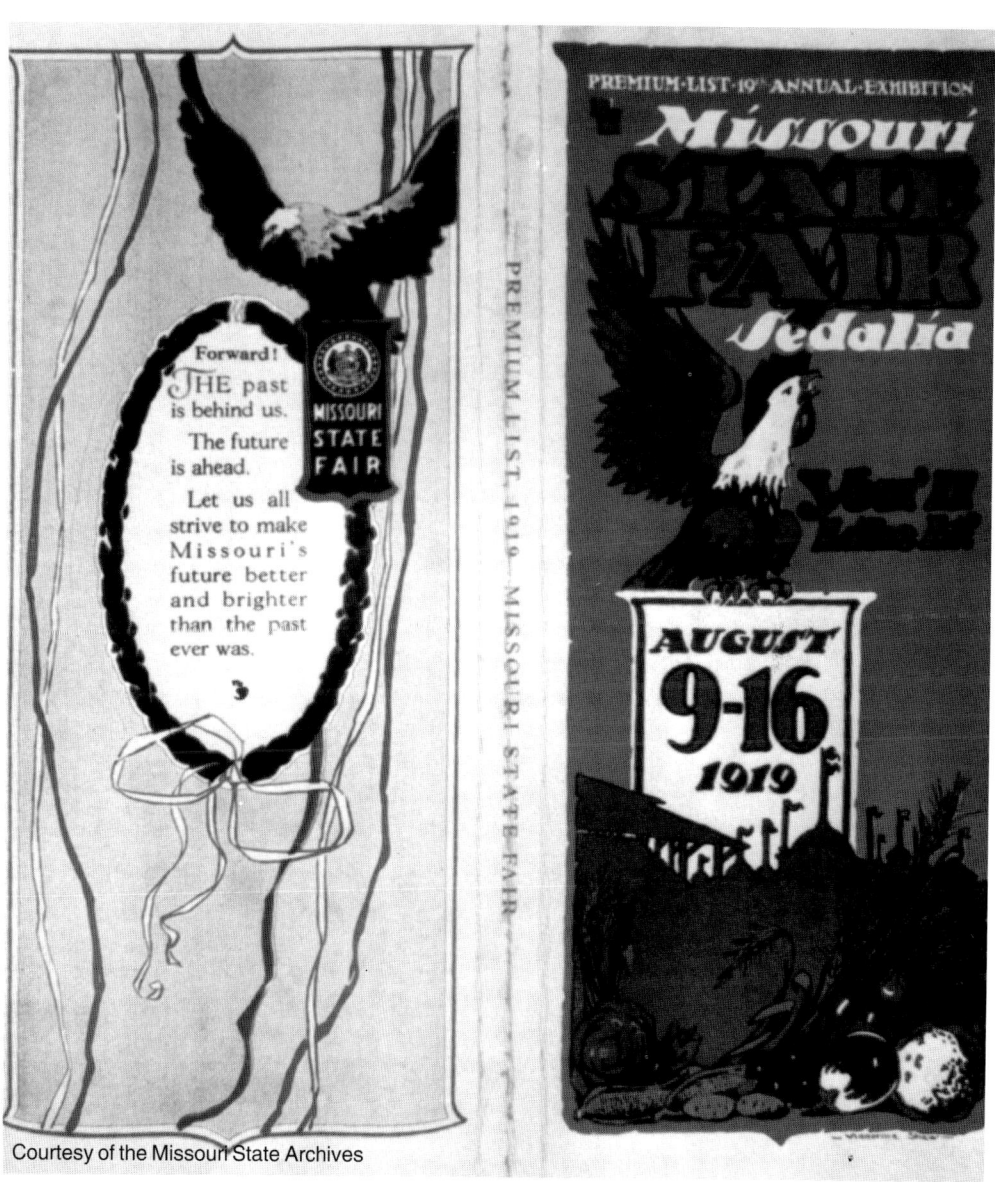

Cover for the 1919 Premium Fair Book.

This was the cover for the 1921 Fair Premium Book. We were also celebrating our State's 100th year of Statehood that year.

Promotional Poster for the 1916 Fair.

The Dorn-Cloney Laundry featured this ad in 1936 to make distant fair visitors aware of their service of keeping everyone looking "spiffy" for the annual event.

WELCOME

State Fair Visitors

It always pays to Look your best!

SUMMER SUITS WASHED **50c**

SUMMER PANTS WASHED **25c**

Our plant and processing by filter pressure is one of the most modern and complete in the middle West. Phone 126 for delivery service.

DORN-CLONEY LAUNDRY & DRY CLEANING CO.
PHONE 126

Courtesy of the Missouri State Archives

In 1923 there was a State Fair Fashion Show staged for the ladies and a St. Louis based clothing company had a booth in what was termed the Automobile Building.

Courtesy of the Missouri State Archives

Fair advertisement from 1917

Fair Dates

1901 September 9-13
1902 August 18-23
1903 August 17-22
1904 August 15-19
1905 August 21-26
1906 September 29 - October 5
1907 October 5-11
1908 October 3-9
1909 October 2-8 *(City of Sedalia's 50th Anniversary - Dan Patch was a big attraction this year)*
1910 October 1-7
1911 September 30 - October 6 *(President Taft came this year)*
1912 September 28 - October 4
1913 September 27 - October 3
1914 September 26 - October 3
1915 September 25 - October 2
1916 September 23-30
1917 September 22-29
1918 August 10-17
1919 August 9-16
1920 August 14-21
1921 August 8-20 *(State Centennial Celebration)*
1922 August 19-26
1923 August 18-25
1924 August 16-23
1925 August 15-22
1926 August 14-21
1927 August 20-27
1928 August 18-25
1929 August 17-24
1930 August 16-23
1931 August 22-29
1932 August 20-27
1933 August 12-19
1934 August 11-18
1935 August 10-17
1936 August 22-29
1937 August 21-28
1938 August 20-27
1939 August 19-26
1940 August 18-25
1941 August 17-24
1942 August 23-30
1943 No Fair (World War II)
1944 No Fair (World War II)
1945 August 19-26
1946 August 18-25
1947 August 17-24
1948 August 22-29
1949 August 21-28

1950 August 20-27
1951 August 18-26 *(1st Governor's Ham Breakfast)*
1952 August 16-24 *(Fair's Golden Anniversary - Year of the Tornado)*
1953 August 22-30
1954 August 21-29
1955 August 20-28 *(President Truman at the Fair)*
1956 August 18-26
1957 August 17-25
1958 August 16-24
1959 August 22-30
1960 August 20-28
1961 August 19-27
1962 August 18-26
1963 August 17-25
1964 August 22-30
1965 August 21-29
1966 August 20-28
1967 August 19-27
1968 August 17-25
1969 August 16-24
1970 August 22-30
1971 August 21-29 *(150 Years of Statehood)*
1972 August 18-27
1973 August 17-26
1974 August 16-25
1975 August 15-24
1976 August 20-29
1977 August 19-28
1978 August 18-27
1979 August 17-26
1980 August 15-24
1981 August 21-30
1982 August 19-29
1983 August 11-21
1984 August 16-25 *(President Reagan at the Fair)*
1985 August 15-24
1986 August 15-24
1987 August 20-30
1988 August 18-28
1989 August 17-27
1990 August 16-26
1991 August 15-25
1992 August 20-30
1993 August 19-29
1994 August 18-28
1995 August 17-27
1996 August 15-24
1997 August 14-23
1998 August 13-23
1999 August 12-22
2000 August 10-20
2001 August 9-19
2002 August 8-18 *(100th Anniversary of the MO State Fair)*

Directors of the Missouri State Fair
1901 to 2002

1901-1907
J.R. Rippey

1908-1914
John T. Stinson

1915-1916
E.T. Major

1917-1921
E.G. Bylander

1922-1932
W.D. Smith

1933-1941
Charles W. Green

1942-1945
Ernest W. Baker

1946-1950
Roy S. Kemper

1951
W.E. "Bill" Preston

1954-1955
Ross Ewing

1956
W.H. Ritzethaler

1957-1960
"Colie" Ervin

1961-1964
W.H. Ritzethaler

1965-1972
W.C. Askew

1973-1974
Ron Jones

1975-1977
Jerry P. Hermann

1978-1979
H.D. Hurd

1980
R.D. "Russ" Nichols

1981-1985
Marian Lucas

1986-1988
Bill Waddell

1989-1993
Roger Alewell

1994-1996
Bill Arthaud

1997-2000
Gary D. Slater

2001-2002
Mel Willard

Sources

Missouri State Fairgrounds - National Registar Nomination Study

Sedalia Democrat

Sedalia Democrat-Sentinel

Sedalia Evening Sentinel

Missouri Ruralist

Interviews with Maxine Griggs, Lucille Bowers and Charles Ramseyer

Fair Premium Books

Missouri State Archives

West Plains Newspaper

Funk & Wagnall's Encyclopedia